W9-BFH-483

A-Z OF
VEGETABLE VARIETY

A~Z OF
VEGETABLE VARIETY

ARCO PUBLISHING, INC.
New York

Published 1985 by Arco Publishing, Inc.
215 Park Avenue South, New York, NY 10003

© Marshall Cavendish Limited 1985

Library of Congress Cataloging in Publication Data

Includes index.
1. Cookery (Vegetables) I. Arco Publishing.
II. Title: A to Z of vegetable variety.
TX801.A195 1985 641.6′5 84-16864
ISBN 0-668-06337-8
ISBN 0-668-06342-4 (pbk.)

Printed and bound in Hong Kong by
Dai Nippon Printing Company

This volume may not be sold outside of
the United States of America or its territories.

Cook's Notes

The handy hints you've always wanted to know.

TIME
Timing explained –
black symbol means
allow extra time

FREEZING
The essential guide to
dishes which freeze

ECONOMY
Tips to make dishes go
further, or for inexpen-
sive ingredients

WATCHPOINT
Look out for special
advice on tricky methods

DID YOU KNOW
Useful background to
recipes or ingredients

PREPARATION
Tips for techniques,
often with illustrations

SERVING IDEAS
Suggestions for good
accompaniments

VARIATIONS
Interesting ways to alter
the basic dish

COOK'S TIPS
Background
information to help
when you need it

BUYING GUIDE
Guide to selecting
suitable ingredients

PRESSURE COOKING
How to save time with
your pressure cooker

STORAGE
How to store and for
how long

INTRODUCTION

Full of flavor and rich in nutrients, vegetables are not only good for you but can be turned into a great variety of colorful and delicious dishes. The A-Z OF VEGETABLE VARIETY helps you to do just that. Here you will find an enormous range of recipes, from tasty soups and appetizers to satisfying, yet economical, main courses.

Arranged in an easy-to-follow alphabetical format, there is a recipe for every occasion. Simply turn to the vegetable you are interested in and sample the recipes suggested. There is also a comprehensive index to help you find specific recipes.

Each recipe is set out in a simple step-by-step style and is accompanied by Cook's Notes giving all sorts of handy hints, ranging from tips on preparation to serving ideas.

Artichoke and tomato salad

SERVES 4
14 oz can artichoke hearts, drained
4 tomatoes, quartered
3 hard-cooked eggs, quartered
4 oz frozen green beans
salt
lettuce leaves, to serve
freshly ground black pepper

DRESSING
3 tablespoons olive oil
1 tablespoon white wine vinegar
2 teaspoons lemon juice
1 teaspoon superfine sugar

1 Rinse the artichoke hearts under cold running water to remove any salty flavor left over from the can liquid. Drain and pat dry on absorbent kitchen paper, then cut into bite-size pieces and place in a bowl.
2 Using a metal spoon, very carefully fold in the tomatoes and eggs. Cover with plastic wrap and refrigerate.
3 Cook the beans according to package directions in boiling salted water until they are tender but still crisp to the bite. Drain thoroughly and refresh under cold running water. Drain the beans again and let cool.
4 Meanwhile, make the dressing: Place all the dressing ingredients in a screw-top jar with salt and pepper to taste and shake well to mix well together.
5 Halve the cooled beans if they are very large, then mix them into the salad with the dressing. Turn the ingredients over gently to coat thoroughly, cover again with plastic wrap and return to the refrigerate for a further 2 hours.
6 Line a serving dish with lettuce leaves and arrange the salad in the center. Sprinkle a little pepper over the top and serve at once.

Cook's Notes

TIME
The salad will take about 30 minutes to prepare altogether. Allow at least 2 hours chilling time before serving.

SERVING IDEAS
This tasty salad is quite filling: Serve it as a fresh appetizer or with cold meats as a snack or lunch dish.

●175 calories per portion

Artichokes with chicken livers

SERVES 4
1½ lb chicken livers, trimmed (see Preparation)
14 oz can artichoke hearts, drained, halved if large
2 tablespoons margarine or butter
1 large onion, sliced
2 teaspoons dried marjoram
3 tablespoons dry sherry
salt and freshly ground black pepper

1 Melt the margarine in a large skillet, add the onion and sauté gently for 5 minutes until soft and lightly colored.
2 Pat the chicken livers dry on absorbent kitchen paper. Add them to the pan and toss with the onions for about 5 minutes, stirring until they are pink inside. !
3 Add the remaining ingredients and cook for a further 5 minutes until the artichoke hearts are thoroughly heated through. Taste and adjust seasoning if necessary. Serve at once.

Cook's Notes

 TIME
Total preparation and cooking is only 15 minutes.

 PREPARATION
Always take care when preparing chicken livers to remove any pieces of gall, which are dark green and will give the dish an unpleasant, bitter flavor.

 SERVING IDEAS
Serve in the center of a ring of rice, mixed together with a little chopped, canned red pimiento for extra color.

! **WATCHPOINT**
Avoid overcooking the livers at this stage or they will be tough and rubbery in texture.

●320 calories per portion

Asparagus in aspic

SERVES 6

1 ½ lb asparagus stalks (see Buying
  guide)
salt
1 sweet red pepper, seeded and cut
  in ½ inch cubes
1 bunch scallions, sliced in rounds
2 cups water
1 tablespoon unflavored gelatin
tarragon sprigs, for garnish

MAYONNAISE

3 tablespoons thick bottled
  mayonnaise
1 tablespoon chopped fresh
  tarragon

1 Trim base of each asparagus
stalk, leaving about 2 inches of the
harder white stem.
2 Put the asparagus in a pan large
enough to hold them lying flat.
Pour over enough boiling water just
to cover and add a pinch of salt.
Cover pan and simmer very gently
for 10-15 minutes until the asparagus stalks are tender.
3 Meanwhile, cook the pepper
cubes and scallions in boiling water
for 4 minutes. Drain.
4 Put 2 tablespoons of the water in
a large bowl, sprinkle over the
gelatin and let soak until spongy.
Bring rest of water to a boil and add
to gelatin, stirring, until it has dissolved. Let cool slightly.
5 Rinse out a deep 6 inch cake pan
with cold water and pour a little of
the gelatin liquid into the base to
make a thin layer. Refrigerate for 15
minutes until set.
6 Carefully drain the asparagus on
absorbent kitchen paper and cut in
1 inch lengths.
7 Arrange a few asparagus tips and
pieces of scallion and red pepper on
top of the gelatin. Spoon over half
remaining gelatin and chill until set
– about 1 hour.
8 Arrange remaining vegetables on
top of the set gelatin and pour in
rest of gelatin. If gelatin has set too
solid, reheat gently first. Refrigerate
for at least 1 hour.
9 Meanwhile, make mayonnaise:
Beat the mayonnaise until it is
creamy, then stir in the tarragon.
10 To serve: Dip base of pan in very
hot water for 2 seconds, then turn
out onto a plate.
11 Garnish with tarragon sprigs
and pass the tarragon mayonnaise
separately.

Cook's Notes

 TIME
30 minutes to make plus
setting time.

 BUYING GUIDE
If fresh asparagus is un-
available, use frozen
asparagus and cook according
to package directions. Alternatively, use a 15 oz can asparagus:
Simply drain and cut in 1 inch
lengths.

● 85 calories per portion

Asparagus pizza

SERVES 4-6
1 cup wholewheat flour
1 cup all-purpose flour
1 teaspoon dried basil
1 teaspoon dried parsley
salt and freshly ground black
    pepper
1 teaspoon easy-blend active dry
    yeast
⅔ cup hand-hot water
margarine, for greasing

TOPPING
2 tablespoons olive oil
1 large onion, minced
1 clove garlic, minced (optional)
14 oz can tomatoes
1 teaspoon dried oregano
2 tablespoons tomato paste
1 cup finely sliced mushrooms
½ lb chorizo sausage, thinly sliced
    (see Buying guide)
15 oz can asparagus spears, drained
6 oz Mozzarella cheese, thinly
    sliced
good pinch each of dried basil,
    parsley and oregano, for
    sprinkling

1 Grease a large baking sheet or pizza pan with margarine.
2 Make the pizza base: Combine the flours in a large bowl. Stir in the basil and parsley and season with salt and pepper. Stir in the yeast.
3 Make a well in the center of the flour mixture and stir in water. Mix together to form a stiff dough.
4 Press the dough into a large circle and put on the prepared baking sheet. Cover with plastic wrap and leave in a warm place for 30 minutes until the dough has slightly risen.
5 Preheat the oven to 425°.
6 Meanwhile, make the topping: Heat the oil in a small saucepan, add the onion and garlic, if using, and sauté gently for 5 minutes until soft and lightly colored. Add the tomatoes, oregano and the tomato paste and season to taste with salt and pepper. Stir in the mixture well, bring to a boil then reduce heat and simmer, uncovered, for 30 minutes, or until thick and slightly reduced, stirring occasionally.
7 Uncover the risen dough and

spread the tomato sauce over it. Put the mushrooms on top, then the sausage slices and then the asparagus spears, arranged like the spokes of a wheel. Place slices of Mozzarella between the asparagus and sprinkle with more herbs.
8 Bake in the oven for 30 minutes or until the cheese has melted and the base is crisp. Serve at once.

Cook's Notes

TIME
Preparation and cooking of the pizza take about 1¼ hours.

BUYING GUIDE
Spanish chorizo sausage is available at many delicatessens and also at large supermarkets. If the chorizo is difficult to obtain, use another cooked spicy sausage. Bierwurst, kabanos or garlic sausage would be ideal.

●735 calories per portion

7

Asparagus and tomato layer

SERVES 4

1½ lb asparagus stalks (see Buying guide)
salt
1 lb tomatoes, peeled and sliced
1 tablespoon chopped fresh basil or parsley
freshly ground black pepper
3 tablespoons butter
½ cup shredded Cheddar cheese

1 Preheat the oven to 375°.
2 Wash the asparagus stalks well in cold water, then trim the base of each spear leaving about ¾ inch of harder white stem.
3 Put the asparagus in a pan large enough to hold them lying flat. Pour over enough boiling water just to cover the asparagus and add a good pinch of salt. Cover the pan and simmer very gently for 10 minutes until semi-cooked.
4 Lift out the asparagus very carefully with a slotted spatula and drain on absorbent kitchen paper.
5 Put half the asparagus in a shallow flameproof serving dish. Arrange half the sliced tomatoes over the asparagus, then sprinkle with half the basil and salt and pepper to taste. Dot with the butter. Layer the remaining asparagus and tomatoes on top and sprinkle with the remaining basil. Season to taste with salt and pepper.
6 Sprinkle the cheese over the top and cook in the oven for 30 minutes. Serve at once.

Cook's Notes

 TIME
30 minutes preparation, 30 minutes cooking.

 BUYING GUIDE
Frozen asparagus may be used if fresh is unavailable – thaw first.

 SERVING IDEAS
This dish makes a luxurious appetizer or a rather special light lunch dish. Brown bread rolls are the only accompaniment needed.

●170 calories per portion

Bean and apricot salad

SERVES 4-6
½ cup dried apricots
1 teaspoon grated orange rind
salt
1 lb fresh English runner beans,
  thinly sliced diagonally, or
  frozen sliced green beans
7 oz can whole kernel corn, drained
3 walnuts, shelled and halved for
  garnish

DRESSING
1 tablespoon orange juice
1 tablespoon olive oil
1 teaspoon honey
freshly ground black pepper
few drops of lemon juice (optional)

1 Cover the apricots with cold water and let stand for 3 hours.
2 Place the apricots and the water in a pan and bring to a boil then cover and simmer for 5-10 minutes until the apricots are just soft. Drain, then cut each apricot lengthwise into 3 strips and mix with the orange rind in a salad bowl.
3 Bring a pan of salted water to a boil and add the beans. Lower the heat and simmer for 5 minutes if fresh and 2 minutes if frozen, until the beans are just tender.
4 Drain and rinse the beans in cold water and drain well again. Add to the apricots, together with the whole kernel corn, and mix.
5 To make the dressing: In a bowl, beat together the orange juice, olive oil, honey, and salt and pepper to taste. Pour the dressing over the salad. Check the seasoning and add

a few drops of lemon if wished.
6 Cover with plastic wrap and chill in the refrigerator for 30 minutes or until ready to serve.
7 To serve: Toss the salad again, and garnish with walnut halves.

Cook's Notes

 TIME
Preparation 30 minutes plus 3 hours to soak apricots; 30 minutes chilling.

 SERVING IDEAS
Serve with cold meats, such as pork or duck or make the salad into a main meal dish by adding ½ lb cooked chicken with the apricots and corn.

● 150 calories per portion

Bean and avocado salad

SERVES 4

1⅓ cups shelled fresh or frozen
   lima beans (see Buying guide
   and Cook's tips)
salt
1 large avocado
4 tomatoes, thinly sliced

DRESSING

1 tablespoon wine vinegar
2 teaspoons water
1 teaspoon superfine sugar
3 tablespoons vegetable oil
good pinch each of freshly ground
   black pepper and dry mustard
1 teaspoon minced onion
1 teaspoon minced mint or
   ½ teaspoon dried

1 Bring a pan of salted water to a boil and cook the fresh lima beans, if using, for 15-20 minutes, until tender. If using frozen beans, cook according to package directions. Drain well and let cool completely (see Cook's tips).
2 Halve, seed and pare the avocado. Cut the flesh in ½ in. dice and put into a bowl together with the lima beans.
3 To make the dressing: Place all the ingredients in a screw-top jar and shake thoroughly until well blended. Pour the dressing over the avocado and lima beans and toss to mix well.
4 Arrange the sliced tomatoes in a border around a serving plate and pile the prepared salad in the center. Serve at once.

Cook's Notes

TIME
Cooking the lima beans takes 15-20 minutes. Allow 30 minutes for cooling. Preparing the salad then takes 10 minutes.

BUYING GUIDE
Yield from beans can vary considerably but 2 lb lima beans in the pod should give you enough for this particular recipe.

COOK'S TIPS
Wear rubber gloves when shelling lima beans or they may stain your hands.
   When using larger, older beans, remove their skins after cooking and cooling, to leave a bright green, tender bean.

SERVING IDEAS
Serve the salad on individual dishes as an appetizer or serve as a side salad with broiled meats or fish. If liked, garnish the top of the salad with chopped hard-cooked egg.

WATCHPOINT
Serve as soon as possible after preparation, or the avocado may start to discolor.

● 285 calories per portion

Bean fiesta

SERVES 4

¾ lb English runner beans, thinly sliced in 1 inch lengths, thawed if frozen
salt
2 tablespoons margarine or butter
1 medium onion, finely chopped
⅓ cup seedless raisins
¼ cup shelled hazelnuts, halved
freshly ground black pepper

1 Cook the beans for 5-7 minutes in boiling salted water until just tender, but still crisp. If using frozen beans, cook according to package directions, making sure they are undercooked rather than overcooked. Drain thoroughly.
2 Melt the margarine in a saucepan, add the onion and cover the pan. Cook over gentle heat until the onion is soft and translucent. Add the raisins and hazelnuts and stir for 2-3 minutes until just heated through. ⚠
3 Add the drained beans to the pan and stir for a further 2 minutes until thoroughly coated. Season with pepper and serve at once.

Cook's Notes

TIME
Preparation time 10-15 minutes, cooking 10 minutes.

SERVING IDEAS
Serve with any simply cooked meat or fish, such as broiled lamb or pork chops or poached or baked fish steaks.

! WATCHPOINT
Do not fry the hazelnuts for too long or they will become soft.

● 125 calories per portion

Beans in green sauce

SERVES 4
1 lb shelled lima beans
sprig of fresh rosemary or pinch of dried
salt

SAUCE
2 tablespoons margarine or butter
3 tablespoons all-purpose flour
⅔ cup milk
4 tablespoons finely chopped fresh parsley
freshly ground black pepper
sprigs of parsley, for garnish

1 Preheat the oven to 225°. Put the beans into a large saucepan and add the rosemary with a pinch of salt. Pour over boiling water to just cover.

2 Cover the pan, bring to a boil, reduce heat and simmer gently for 5-10 minutes until tender (see Cook's tips.)

3 Drain the beans, reserving ⅔ cup of the cooking water and discarding the sprig of rosemary, if used. Put the beans in a warmed serving dish and keep warm in the oven.

4 Make the sauce: Melt the margarine in a small saucepan, sprinkle in the flour and stir over low heat for 1-2 minutes until straw-colored. Remove from the heat and gradually stir in the milk and reserved cooking water. Return to the heat and simmer, stirring, until the sauce is thick and smooth.

5 Stir the chopped parsley into the sauce and season to taste with salt and pepper. Simmer the sauce gently, stirring constantly for 2 minutes (see Cook's tips).

6 Pour the green sauce over the lima beans in the dish and serve hot, garnished with parsley sprigs.

Cook's Notes

 TIME
Preparation takes about 15 minutes, if using fresh beans. Cooking takes about 15 minutes.

 SERVING IDEAS
Serve lima beans in green sauce with a boiled or baked ham roast, with broiled ham steaks or sliced cooked ham. They are also good with lamb roast.

COOK'S TIPS
If using frozen lima beans, cook according to package directions.

For a more evenly colored sauce, process in a blender until smooth and green. Reheat.

● 175 calories per portion

Beans with peaches

SERVES 4
2 lb lima beans (unshelled weight)
   or 1 lb frozen
salt
large sprig fresh mint
3 fresh peaches, peeled (see
   Preparation)
mint sprigs, for garnish

DRESSING
2 tablespoons olive or sunflower
   oil
1 tablespoon white wine vinegar
2 tablespoons finely chopped fresh
   parsley or coriander
freshly ground black pepper

1 Bring a large pan of salted water to a boil, add the beans and mint and bring back to a boil. Lower the heat slightly and simmer for about 6 minutes until just tender.
2 Meanwhile, make the dressing:

 Cook's Notes

 TIME
Preparation and cooking take about 25 minutes, but allow at least 1 hour for cooling.

 VARIATION
Use 14 oz can drained peach slices instead of fresh peaches.

 PREPARATION
To peel the peaches, immerse in very hot water for 1 minute. Drain, then cut the peel near the stalk and remove the peel.

 SERVING IDEAS
This salad is particularly good with lamb roast, lamb chops or broiled ham steaks. When serving with hot roast meat, try thickening the dressing with 2 tablespoons plain yogurt and adding minced garlic for extra flavor.

! WATCHPOINT
The beans should still be hot when added so that they absorb the flavor of the dressing.

●175 calories per portion

Pour the oil into a large bowl, add the vinegar, parsley and salt and pepper to taste, then mix well together with a fork.
3 Drain the beans thoroughly, then immediately put them into the bowl of dressing. [!] Toss well to combine, then cover and leave for at

least 1 hour until completely cold.
4 Just before serving, slice the peaches very thinly, then gently stir them into the cold beans. Taste and adjust seasoning, if necessary. Transfer salad to a serving bowl, garnish with mint and serve at once, while peaches are still firm.

Beans pickled with herbs

MAKES 1 LB

1 lb green beans, trimmed (see Buying guide)
2½ cups white wine vinegar
1 small onion, thinly sliced
1 tablespoon sugar
2 tablespoons whole black peppercorns
2 bay leaves
1 blade whole mace
1 large sprig of fresh thyme, oregano or tarragon
5 cups water
1 tablespoon salt

1 Sterilize 2 jars (see Cook's tips): Wash and thoroughly rinse them, then stand on a rack in a large pan of water and bring to a boil. Remove the jars from the pan, stand upside down to drain, then put in a warm oven to dry.
2 Pour the vinegar into a large stainless steel or enameled pan – the vinegar has an acid content so the pan must be non-corrosive.
3 Add the onion, sugar, black peppercorns, bay leaves, mace and thyme. Bring to a boil, cover the pan and boil for 1 minute, then remove from heat and let cool.
4 Blanch the beans: Pour the water into a large saucepan and add the salt. Bring to a boil, add the beans (see Cook's tips) and simmer for 2-3 minutes until bright green in color and just tender.
5 Immediately drain the beans in a colander and rinse under cold running water to cool quickly. Pat dry with a clean dish towel. Pack the beans upright in the sterilized jars.
6 Strain the vinegar mixture into the jars to cover the beans.
7 Seal tightly with vinegar-proof lids. Label and store in a cool, dry place (see Storage).

Cook's Notes

 TIME
About 35 minutes preparation and cooking, plus cooling and storage.

 SERVING IDEAS
Serve with cold meats, or as part of a salad or mixed hors d'oeuvre platter.

 BUYING GUIDE
Only pickle young, fresh beans that are in prime condition.

 STORAGE
The pickled beans are best left for at least 2 months to mature.

COOK'S TIPS
Screw-top instant coffee jars, that are about 6 inches tall, are an ideal shape for green beans. The plastic-lined lids are vinegar proof. Each jar holds ½ lb fresh beans.

For a crunchier pickle, the beans may be pickled without blanching, but they must be soaked for 24 hours in a brine solution, made of 2 oz salt and 2½ cups of water, before bottling. After soaking, rinse thoroughly under cold running water, then pat dry with a clean dish towel.

●65 calories per jar

Beans in sunset sauce

SERVES 4-6

1 lb green beans, thawed if frozen, cut diagonally in 2 inch slices (see Watchpoint)
2 tablespoons finely chopped parsley (optional)

SAUCE

8 tiny pearl onions or 3 shallots, quartered
⅞ cup water
¼ cup tomato paste
¼ cup olive oil
2 tablespoons fresh orange juice
3 tablespoons dry cider
1 clove garlic, minced (optional)
8-12 coriander seeds, lightly crushed (see Preparation)
6 black peppercorns, lightly crushed
salt
1 strip thinly pared orange rind

1 Put all sauce ingredients into a small pan. Bring to a boil, skim off any foam and lower the heat. Simmer, uncovered, for 20 minutes.

2 Add the sliced beans to the pan, bring back just to the simmering point and simmer the beans for 20-30 minutes, until they are just tender (see Cook's tips). Discard the orange rind and adjust seasoning if necessary (see Cook's tips).
3 Transfer the beans with the sauce to a warmed dish. Sprinkle with parsley, if liked, and serve.

Cook's Notes

 TIME
Preparation, if using fresh beans, takes about 10 minutes. Cooking, including making the sauce, takes 40-50 minutes.

 WATCHPOINT
It is very important to cut the beans into even-size pieces, so that they cook evenly.

 COOK'S TIPS
If using frozen beans, simmer them in the sauce for only 10 minutes.
If the sauce seems a little too runny, transfer the beans to a warmed serving dish, using a slotted spoon, and keep hot. Increase the heat and bring the sauce in the pan to a boil. Boil for 3-4 minutes to reduce slightly and thicken, then pour over the beans and stir to mix well. Serve at once.

 PREPARATION
To release more of their flavor, lightly crush the coriander seeds and peppercorns, but do not grind them to a powder. Use a pestle and mortar if you have one, or put them in a plastic or brown paper bag and tap them gently with a rolling pin.

 SERVING IDEAS
This is a special occasion way of cooking green beans, and is ideal as an accompaniment to meat dishes such as roasts or broils which do not have their own sauce.

●165 calories per portion

Beet and orange salad

SERVES 4
4 cooked beet, peeled and sliced
2 oranges, peeled (see Buying guide and Preparation)
1 head lettuce, leaves separated
2 large tomatoes, sliced
3-4 teaspoons finely chopped walnuts

DRESSING
1 teaspoon minced onion
1 teaspoon chopped chives
good pinch of salt
½ teaspoon prepared English mustard
good pinch of superfine sugar
freshly ground black pepper
3 tablespoons olive or vegetable oil
1 tablespoon wine vinegar
dash of Worcestershire sauce

1 Cut the orange into thin rings and set aside.
2 Arrange the lettuce leaves on a salad platter.
3 Arrange the orange and beet slices alternately in a ring on top of the lettuce. Arrange overlapping slices of tomato in the center of the dish and sprinkle with the finely chopped walnuts.
4 Make the dressing: Put the reserved orange juice from the peeled oranges in a bowl. Add the onion and chives to the bowl, together with the salt, mustard, sugar and pepper to taste. Mix well together with a fork. Add the oil, vinegar and Worcestershire and beat together until well blended.
5 Spoon the prepared dressing over the salad and serve at once.

Cook's Notes

 TIME
This unusual salad takes 20 minutes preparation.

 BUYING GUIDE
Choose thin-skinned seedless oranges as these will look more attractive in the finished salad, and are much easier to cut into even slices.

 PREPARATION
Peel the oranges over a bowl to catch the juices; reserve the juice. When peeling, use a fine serrated knife and a sawing action so that the rind is removed together with the pith and white membrane in a single clean cut.

 COOK'S TIP
Do not prepare too soon in advance or the beet may discolor the oranges and spoil the overall effect.

 SERVING IDEAS
Serve as a side salad with broiled fish or poultry, or as part of a salad buffet.

 VARIATIONS
Use a herb-flavored vinegar, such as tarragon or mint vinegar for the dressing. Use chopped hazelnuts or salted peanuts instead of the walnuts.

● 150 calories per portion

Broccoli with egg

SERVES 4
1 lb broccoli (see Buying guide)
salt
¼ cup butter
1 cup soft white bread crumbs
2 hard-cooked eggs, finely chopped
   (see Preparation)
finely grated rind and juice of ½
   lemon
1 tablespoon finely chopped fresh
   parsley
freshly ground black pepper

1 Divide the broccoli into stalks leaving small leaves attached.
2 Bring a pan of salted water to a boil, add the broccoli (see Cook's tip), cover and simmer for about 5 minutes until the broccoli is tender but not soft.
3 Meanwhile, make the topping: Melt the butter in a skillet, add the bread crumbs and sauté over moderate heat, stirring, for about 5 minutes.
4 Add the finely chopped eggs to the fried crumbs together with the lemon rind and juice, parsley and salt and pepper to taste. Cook gently for 1-2 minutes until heated through.
5 Drain the broccoli thoroughly and transfer to a warmed serving dish. Sprinkle the topping over the broccoli and serve at once.

Cook's Notes

 TIME
20 minutes preparation including hard-cooking the eggs; 10 minutes cooking.

 SERVING IDEAS
The lemony flavor of this dish goes well with fish, veal and chicken dishes. The color provides a good contrast for these light meats.

 COOK'S TIP
Try and arrange the broccoli stalks in the saucepan so that the stalks are immersed in the water and the heads are just above the water, cooking in the steam.

 BUYING GUIDE
You can use any of the broccoli family for this recipe: Try calabrese or cauliflower.

 PREPARATION
Hard-cook the eggs for 10 minutes, and then immediately hold under cold running water, and tap the shells against the side of the sink to crack them. This will stop further cooking and prevent a dark rim from forming around the egg yolks, which is caused by over-cooking.

●180 calories per portion

Broccoli and peppers

SERVES 4
1 lb frozen broccoli, thawed and drained
1 sweet red pepper, seeded and cut in thin strips
2 tablespoons vegetable oil
1 clove garlic, minced (optional)
salt and freshly ground black pepper
2 tablespoons butter

1 Divide the broccoli into smaller flowerets, by slicing lengthwise through the stalks.

Cook's Notes

TIME
Preparation and cooking take 20 minutes.

WATCHPOINT
If overcooked the broccoli will be soggy.

COOK'S TIP
Use fresh broccoli if available. Cook in salted water for 3 minutes, then drain thoroughly before sautéing.

VARIATION
Sprinkle with ½ cup grated Parmesan cheese.

●140 calories per portion

2 Heat the oil in a large heavy-bottomed skillet, add the pepper and garlic, if using, and gently sauté for 5-10 minutes.
3 Increase the heat to moderate, add the broccoli, season with salt and pepper to taste and sauté, stirring constantly, for 5-6 minutes [!] until just cooked through.
4 Transfer the vegetables to a warmed serving dish and dot with the butter. Serve at once.

Brussels sprouts sweet and sour

SERVES 4
1¼ lb fresh Brussels sprouts (see Buying guide), or 1 lb frozen
¼ cup margarine or butter
1 medium onion, minced
2 Newtown Pippin apples
2 tablespoons seedless raisins
3 tablespoons lemon juice (see Cook's tip)
3 tablespoons honey
salt and freshly ground black pepper

1 Cook the sprouts in boiling salted water for about 10-15 minutes until just tender. If using frozen sprouts, cook according to the package directions.
2 Meanwhile, melt the margarine in a saucepan, add the onion and sauté gently until soft but not colored. Pare, core and chop the apples fairly coarsely, then add to the onion with the raisins. Stir well. Season well with salt and pepper.
3 Mix together the lemon juice and honey; pour into a small pitcher.

4 When the sprouts are cooked, drain well, add to onion mixture and stir well to mix. Transfer to a serving bowl, pour over the sauce and serve.

Cook's Notes

 TIME
Total preparation and cooking time, if using fresh sprouts, is 25 minutes.

 VARIATIONS
Broccoli may be substituted for Brussels sprouts and any other crisp dessert apple such as a Jonathan or McIntosh may be used instead of Newtown Pippin.

 COOK'S TIP
The average lemon yields 2 tablespoons of juice, so for this recipe you will need 1½ lemons.

 BUYING GUIDE
When buying Brussels sprouts, choose ones which are small, compact and a good green color with no signs of yellowing. If buying sprouts packed in a plastic bag from a supermarket, make sure there are no signs of mold on them.

 SERVING IDEAS
You can serve this unusual dish of Brussels sprouts in place of ordinary boiled sprouts with roast or broiled meats.

●190 calories per portion

Cabbage and lemon sauce

SERVES 4-6
1 large head green cabbage, finely sliced
salt

SAUCE
1½ tablespoons margarine or butter
1½ tablespoons all-purpose flour
1¼ cups warm milk
grated rind and juice of 1 large lemon
freshly grated nutmeg
freshly ground black pepper
lemon slices and 2 teaspoons chopped chives, for garnish

1 Bring a saucepan of salted water to a boil.
2 Meanwhile, make the sauce: Melt the margarine in a separate saucepan, sprinkle in the flour and stir over low heat for 1-2 minutes until straw-colored. Remove from the heat and gradually stir in the milk. Return to heat and simmer, stirring, until thickened and smooth.
3 Plunge the cabbage into the boiling water and boil gently for 5 minutes, stirring frequently.
4 Stir the lemon rind and juice into the sauce, then season to taste with freshly grated nutmeg, and plenty of salt and pepper (see Cook's tip).
5 Drain the cabbage well, then return to the rinsed-out pan. Pour in the sauce, then toss over gentle heat until the cabbage is lightly coated in the sauce. [!]
6 Turn into a warmed serving dish. Garnish with the lemon slices and chives and serve at once.

Cook's Notes

 TIME
Preparation 10 minutes, cooking 10 minutes.

 COOK'S TIP
The sauce needs plenty of salt to bring out the lemon flavor.

 WATCHPOINT
It is essential that the cabbage is tossed quickly in the sauce, so that it still has a "bite" to it. Do not overcook it at this stage, or the finished dish will be soggy.

 VARIATIONS
If chives are not available, use finely chopped scallion tops instead. Or use fresh tarragon if available.

 SERVING IDEAS
The lemon sauce makes this a delicious accompaniment to poached, broiled or fried white fish.
It is also good with a lamb roast or broiled lamb chops or with country-style pork ribs.

● 125 calories per portion

Carrot meat roll

SERVES 4-6
1½ lb lean ground beef
1 large slice bread, crust removed
2 eggs, beaten
1 onion, minced
salt and freshly ground black pepper
3 tablespoons tomato catsup
4 teaspoons soft light brown sugar
2 cups grated carrot
1 cup soft bread crumbs
4 tablespoons chopped parsley
cauliflower flowerets, stuffed
   green olives and parsley, for
   garnish

1 Preheat the oven to 350°, and cut out a piece of extra wide foil about 18 × 16 inches.
2 Put the bread in a shallow dish and pour over a little water. Let soak, then squeeze out water. Crumble the bread into the beef in a bowl.
3 Add half the beaten eggs, together with the onion, salt and pepper. Mix well (see Cook's tip).
4 Turn the meat mixture onto the center of the foil and pat it out to a rectangle 13 × 10 × ½ inch.
5 Mix the catsup with the brown sugar in a bowl and brush half the mixture over the meat.
6 In another bowl, mix the grated carrots with the bread crumbs, parsley, the remaining egg, and season with salt and pepper. Spread the mixture over the meat and, with your hands, pat it down evenly.
7 Using the foil to help, and starting from a short edge, roll up the meat like a jelly roll. Smooth away any cracks that appear in the meat as you roll it up. Slide the roll to the center of the foil and seal the 2 short edges of foil together, leaving space around the roll (see Preparation). Seal the ends of the foil in the same way. Lift into a roasting pan.
8 Bake in the oven for 1 hour. Fold back the foil and brush the roll with the remaining catsup mixture. Return to oven, uncovered, on a high shelf, for 15 minutes.
9 Using 2 slotted spatulas, carefully transfer the meat roll to a warmed serving dish. Garnish roll with cauliflower, olives and parsley.

Cook's Notes

 TIME
Preparation takes 45 minutes; cooking 1¼ hours.

 WATCHPOINT
It is important to pack the meat mixture firmly when making the rectangle shape on the foil otherwise there will be a lot of cracks on the outside surface and the meat roll will fall apart as it cooks.

COOK'S TIP
When mixing ground beef with other ingredients the best utensil is your hand – squeeze the meat into the other ingredients until thoroughly combined.

PREPARATION
To roll up the meat in foil:

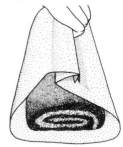

Carefully slide the meat roll back to the center of the foil and bring the 2 short edges of foil together above the roll. Leaving space around the roll, seal the short edges tightly.

●570 calories per portion

Carrot and rice soup

SERVES 4-8
1½ lb baby carrots, thinly sliced
2 tablespoons margarine or butter
2½ cups chicken broth
1 teaspoon sugar
salt and freshly ground black pepper
⅔ cup milk
¾ cup cooked rice (see Cook's tips)
4 eggs at room temperature (see
    Cook's tips)
2 scallions, minced
⅔ cup light cream

1 Melt the margarine in a saucepan, add the carrots and sauté gently for 2-3 minutes to soften slightly.
2 Add the chicken broth and sugar and season to taste with salt and pepper. Bring to a boil, then lower the heat and simmer, uncovered, for 3 minutes or until the carrots are very tender.
3 Remove the pan from the heat and let mixture cool slightly, then pour it into the goblet of a blender and work for a few seconds until smooth. Return the purée to the rinsed-out pan and stir in the milk and the cooked rice. Taste and adjust the seasoning, with salt and pepper, if necessary.
4 Heat the soup gently until hot but not boiling, then break in the eggs and poach them for about 8 minutes or until they are firm enough to be lifted out with a slotted spoon.
5 Spoon an egg into each of 4 warmed soup bowls and pour over the soup. Sprinkle over the minced scallions, then swirl a little light cream into each serving. Serve the soup at once.

Cook's Notes

TIME
Preparation takes 15 minutes, cooking takes about 15 minutes.

SERVING IDEAS
This is a fairly substantial soup, so serve with a light accompaniment such as Melba toast or a selection of crackers.

COOK'S TIPS
If cooking raw rice for this dish, you will need 2 tablespoons to provide ¾ cup cooked rice.

Remove the eggs from the refrigerator 1 hour before using: Cold eggs will require a longer time to set.

●155 calories per portion

Carrot ring

SERVES 4-6
2 lb carrots, thinly sliced
salt
2 tablespoons margarine or butter
⅔ cup chicken broth
1 egg, beaten
½ cup shredded Cheddar cheese
freshly ground black pepper
generous pinch of nutmeg
generous squeeze of lemon juice
margarine, for greasing

1 Preheat the oven to 350°. Grease a 3-cup ring mold thoroughly (see Cook's tips).
2 Bring a pan of salted water to a boil and cook the carrots in it for 10 minutes or until almost tender.
3 Drain well, then add the margarine and broth to the carrots in the pan and simmer, stirring occasionally, for about 10 minutes, until all the liquid has been absorbed. !
4 Mash the carrots thoroughly with the beaten egg and the cheese and season well with pepper, nutmeg and lemon juice.
5 Transfer the carrot mixture to the ring mold. Press down well and smooth the top.
6 Bake in the oven for 30 minutes until set (it should be firm to the touch).
7 To unmold: Run a knife round the edge, then invert a warmed serving plate on top and give a sharp jerk to unmold. Serve the carrot ring at once.

Cook's Notes

 TIME
Preparation and pre-cooking take 30 minutes; cooking time is 30 minutes.

 SERVING IDEAS
Pile freshly cooked green peas or sprigs of watercress into the center of the ring and around the base, if wished. The ring would make a spectacularly different vegetable dish for a dinner party.

 VARIATIONS
Use parsnips or rutabagas, cut into small dice, in place of the carrots, or try a mixture of the root vegetables.

 COOK'S TIPS
Be sure to use an oven-proof ring mold, not a mold suitable only for cold mixtures such as mousses.
Cooking time for carrots varies enormously depending on the season. Old carrots will take longer to cook than the time given in stage 2.

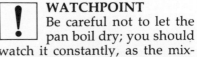 **WATCHPOINT**
Be careful not to let the pan boil dry; you should watch it constantly, as the mixture does not contain much liquid, and may burn.

●180 calories per portion.

Cauliflower with asparagus sauce

SERVES 4
1 lb cauliflower, broken into
    flowerets
salt
hard-cooked egg, chopped, for
    garnish

SAUCE
1 tablespoon margarine
2 tablespoons all-purpose flour
10 oz can asparagus spears, drained
    and liquid reserved
2 tablespoons cold water
3 tablespoons light cream
freshly ground black pepper

1 Bring a pan of salted water to a boil, add the cauliflower flowerets and simmer for about 15 minutes until just tender.

2 Meanwhile, make the sauce: Melt the margarine in a saucepan, sprinkle in the flour and stir over low heat for 1-2 minutes until straw-colored. Mix the asparagus liquid with the water then gradually add to the pan and simmer, stirring, until thick and smooth.

3 Remove from heat and stir in the cream, then add the asparagus spears. Crush the asparagus with a potato masher until well blended into the sauce, then season to taste with salt and pepper. ! Return to heat and heat through gently, stirring with a wooden spoon.

4 Drain the cauliflower well and arrange in a warmed serving dish. Pour the sauce over the cauliflower, garnish with the chopped egg and serve at once.

Cook's Notes

 TIME
This dish takes about 20 minutes to prepare.

 SERVING IDEAS
Serve with broiled pork or chicken.

 WATCHPOINT
Season the asparagus sauce lightly.

●110 calories per portion

Celery and cornmeal flan

SERVES 4
1¼ cups cornmeal (see Did you know)
salt
3 tablespoons vegetable oil
⅔ cup hot water
1 large onion, chopped
3 celery stalks, chopped
1 tablespoon tomato paste
freshly ground black pepper
1 cup shredded Cheddar cheese
4 tomatoes, peeled and sliced
6-8 stuffed olives, sliced
melted margarine, for greasing

1 Preheat the oven to 350°. Grease the base and side of an 8½-9 inch loose-bottomed flan pan.
2 Place the cornmeal, pinch of salt and 2 tablespoons vegetable oil in a bowl and pour on the hot water. Stir well, then mix with your fingers to form a smooth, soft dough.

3 Line the prepared flan pan with the warm dough, gently kneading it into place with your fingers. Set aside to cool.
4 Heat the remaining oil in a skillet. Add the onion and sauté gently for 5 minutes until soft and lightly colored. Add the celery and cook gently for another 10 minutes, stirring occasionally. Stir in the tomato paste and season to taste with salt and pepper.
5 Sprinkle about one-third of the

cheese evenly over the cornmeal base, then add the onion and celery mixture. Top with another third of the cheese. Arrange the sliced tomatoes on top, then sprinkle over the remaining cheese. Bake in the oven for about 35 minutes until the topping is golden.
6 Remove the flan from the oven, arrange the sliced olives decoratively on top, then return to the oven for a further 5 minutes. Remove from pan and serve hot.

Cook's Notes

 TIME
This unusual flan takes 20 minutes to prepare and 40 minutes to cook.

 SERVING IDEAS
Serve with sliced green beans tossed in butter or with a green bean salad. This pie makes a substantial and very tasty lunch dish served with a glass of cider or beer.

? DID YOU KNOW
Cornmeal is a traditional ingredient of both the United States and Latin America – the Indians use it to make both bread and pastry. Cornmeal may be yellow or white; hominy is white flint corn with skinned kernels. Ground hominy is commonly known as hominy grits.

●385 calories per portion

Celery and peanut soup

SERVES 4

4 **large celery stalks, chopped (see Economy)**
6 **tablespoons crunchy peanut butter**
1 **tablespoon margarine or butter**
1 **tablespoon vegetable oil**
1 **onion, chopped**
3 **cups light broth**
salt and freshly ground black pepper
¼ **cup light cream, to serve**
chopped celery leaves, for garnish

1 Melt the margarine in the oil in a saucepan, add the celery and onion and cook gently for 5 minutes until the onion is soft and lightly colored.
2 Add the broth and bring to a boil. Lower the heat, cover and simmer gently for about 30 minutes until the celery is tender.
3 Cool the mixture a little, then work in a blender for a few seconds until smooth.
4 Return to the rinsed-out pan, place over low heat, then beat in the peanut butter. Heat through until just boiling. ✳ Taste and then adjust seasoning.
5 Ladle the soup into 4 warmed individual bowls. Stir 1 tablespoon cream into each, then wait for a few seconds for the cream to rise to the surface. Sprinkle the chopped celery leaves in the center of the bowls and serve at once.

Cook's Notes

TIME
Total preparation and cooking time is about 45 minutes.

FREEZING
Cool quickly, then pour into a rigid container, leaving ¾ inch headspace. Seal, label and freeze for up to 2 months. To serve: Thaw at room temperature for 2 hours, then reheat in a heavy-bottomed pan, stirring frequently until bubbling. Taste and adjust seasoning, then proceed from the beginning of stage 5.

ECONOMY
This is a good way of using up outside celery stalks which may be a little tough, saving the more tender inner stalks for use in salads or serving with cheese.

SERVING IDEAS
Serve with freshly baked bread or rolls – crunchy brown rolls or those coated with a sprinkling of sesame or poppy seeds go particularly well with this soup.

●265 calories per portion

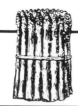

Celery soufflé

SERVES 4
10 oz can condensed celery soup
3 celery stalks, chopped
3 egg yolks
pinch of freshly grated nutmeg
salt and freshly ground black pepper
4 egg whites
1 tablespoon grated Parmesan cheese
margarine, for greasing

1 Preheat the oven to 350°. Grease a 9-cup soufflé mold or ovenproof dish.
2 Pour the celery soup into a saucepan and warm through gently. Stir in the celery.
3 Remove the soup from the heat and stir in the egg yolks and nutmeg. Season to taste with salt and freshly ground black pepper.
4 In a clean, dry bowl beat the egg whites until they are standing in stiff peaks.
5 Using a metal spoon, fold a spoonful of the egg whites into celery mixture and then fold in the remainder of the egg whites.
6 Pour the mixture into the prepared dish and bake in the oven for 40 minutes.
7 Carefully slide the oven shelf out a little way, sprinkle the grated Parmesan over the soufflé and return it to the oven for a further 5 minutes. Serve at once.

Cook's Notes

TIME
This soufflé takes 10 minutes to prepare and 45 minutes to cook.

VARIATIONS
Use can of condensed mushroom soup and some sliced fresh mushrooms instead of the celery soup and celery. Cheddar cheese can be used instead of Parmesan, or the cheese can be omitted altogether, if you prefer.

COOK'S TIP
Reserve the spare egg yolk and add it to a sauce for a savory dish to give it extra richness.

●150 calories per portion

Corn and tuna chowder

SERVES 4-6
12 oz can whole kernel corn
7 oz can tuna fish
2 tablespoons margarine or butter
1 large onion, minced
2 tablespoons all-purpose flour
2 teaspoons paprika
pinch of cayenne
3¾ cups milk
pinch of salt
grated rind of ½ lemon

TO FINISH
½ cup finely shredded Cheddar cheese
4 tablespoons finely chopped parsley

1 Drain the corn, reserving the juice. Drain off the oil from the tuna fish and discard. Place the fish on absorbent kitchen paper to remove excess oil. Using a fork, flake the drained fish into a bowl.

2 Melt the margarine in a saucepan, add the onion and cook gently until soft but not colored.

3 Stir in the flour, paprika and cayenne and cook for 1 minute, stirring constantly with a wooden spoon. Gradually stir in 1¼ cups milk and the reserved corn juice and bring to a boil, stirring.

4 Stir in the remaining milk and bring the mixture to the simmering point. Add the salt and the grated lemon rind.

5 Add the corn and simmer the soup, uncovered, for 5 minutes. Add the tuna fish and simmer for a further 5 minutes until heated through.

6 To finish: Taste and adjust seasoning, then pour into warmed individual soup bowls. Sprinkle with the cheese and parsley and serve at once.

Cook's Notes

TIME
The soup takes 30 minutes to prepare and cook.

COOK'S TIP
To make the soup in advance, prepare it up to the end of stage 4, leave to cool, then refrigerate. To finish: Reheat until bubbling, stirring constantly, then continue from stage 5.

! WATCHPOINTS
It is important to remove as much oil as possible from the tuna fish so that the chowder is not greasy.

Always add the cheese just before serving, when the soup is still hot enough for it to melt. Do not bring back to a boil after adding the cheese or the soup will be stringy.

●410 calories per portion

Corn waffles

MAKES 8-10 WAFFLES
7 oz can whole kernel corn, drained
1½ cups all-purpose flour
1 tablespoon baking powder
2 eggs, separated
1¼ cups milk
6 tablespoons butter, melted
salt and freshly ground black pepper
vegetable oil, for greasing

1 Stir the flour and baking powder into a bowl and make a well in the center. Add the egg yolks and beat thoroughly, gradually working the dry ingredients into the center. Add the milk and melted butter and beat until smooth. Stir in the drained corn and season to taste with salt and pepper.
2 In a clean, dry bowl, beat the egg whites until standing in stiff peaks, then, using a metal spoon, carefully fold into the batter.
3 If you have an electric waffle iron, follow the manufacturer's directions. If your waffle iron is the top-of-the-stove type, as in the picture, lightly grease with oil (see Cook's tips) and set over high heat for about 2 minutes until it is hot, turning occasionally so that both plates are heated. Lower the heat to moderate. Spoon a little batter into the heated waffle iron. Close the lid and cook for 30-60 seconds, then turn the waffle iron over and cook for a further 30-60 seconds until the corn waffle is a light golden brown on both sides (see Cook's tips). Serve at once (see Cook's tips).

Cook's Notes

TIME
Preparation 10 minutes, cooking 10 minutes.

COOK'S TIPS
If you do not have a waffle iron, a lightly oiled griddle or skillet may be used instead. Simply drop tablespoons of the corn mixture onto the griddle or pan and cook for 1-2 minutes, turning the waffles once.

Use the first waffle as a test one to make sure the heat is high enough and the quantity of batter is correct. The number of waffles will depend on the size and shape of the waffle iron used; some types cook 1 waffle at a time, others cook several waffles together.

Waffles are at their best when served immediately but, if they are to be kept hot for a short time, place in a single layer on a wire rack in a low oven. Do not pile them on top of each other or they will become soft.

SERVING IDEAS
These waffles are delicious served for breakfast with broiled bacon.

●210 calories per waffle

Cucumber chicken

SERVES 4

4 chicken breasts, each weighing ½ lb, skinned (see Buying guide)
3 tablespoons all-purpose flour
salt and freshly ground black pepper
¼ cup butter
1 tablespoon vegetable oil
1 cucumber, pared and diced
1 bunch scallions, minced (see Cook's tips)
1¼ cups sour cream
2 tablespoons chopped fresh mint or 2 teaspoons dried mint
finely chopped scallion tops, for garnish

1 Season the flour with salt and pepper and put it on a plate. Coat the chicken breasts thoroughly and evenly all over with the flour.
2 Melt half the butter in the oil in a large skillet over moderate to high heat. Add the chicken breasts and brown them on both sides. Turn down the heat to low and cook the chicken for about 20-25 minutes,

turning occasionally, until the juices run clear when the chicken is pierced in the thickest part with a sharp knife or fine skewer.
3 Meanwhile, bring a saucepan of salted water to a boil, add the diced cucumber and boil gently for 7 minutes. Drain very thoroughly.
4 Melt the remaining butter in a saucepan, add the chopped scallions and sauté gently for 5 minutes. Add the drained cucumber to the pan and mix the vegetables

together with a wooden spoon. Add the sour cream and mint and heat sauce gently for a few minutes until hot. ⚠ Season to taste with salt and pepper.
5 Drain the cooked chicken breasts on absorbent kitchen paper and place on a warmed serving platter. Spoon a little of the cucumber sauce over each chicken breast, to cover partially. Sprinkle with chopped scallion tops. Serve at once, with the sauce passed separately.

Cook's Notes

 TIME
Preparation and cooking take about 40 minutes

 SERVING IDEAS
This is a lovely fresh-tasting dish. Minted tiny new potatoes and buttered carrots would go well with it.

 BUYING GUIDE
Most supermarkets sell fresh chicken breasts from chilling cabinets; try to use these rather than frozen ones. They are moister and tastier.

 COOK'S TIPS
Reserve the trimmed green scallion tops for the garnish.
If you prefer you could use half plain yogurt and half sour cream for the sauce, but bear in mind that it will be a little less thick and creamy.

 WATCHPOINT
Do not let the sauce boil or it may curdle, and the dish will look unattractive.

●475 calories per portion

Cucumber crisp

SERVES 4
1 large cucumber
salt
½ cup shredded Cheddar cheese
½ cup soft white bread crumbs
freshly ground black pepper
2 tablespoons butter
vegetable oil, for greasing

1 Preheat the oven to 400°.
2 Cut the unpared cucumber into pieces about 2 inches long. Cut each piece in half lengthwise, then cut each piece into 4 lengthwise to make long finger shapes. Remove and discard the cucumber seeds if they are very large.
3 Bring a pan of salted water to a boil and cook the cucumber in it for 4 minutes, then drain well.
4 Grease a small ovenproof dish and arrange half the cucumber pieces over the base.
5 Mix together the cheese and bread crumbs and sprinkle half the mixture over the cucumber. Season with black pepper and dot with half the butter.
6 Cover with the remaining cucumber pieces and scatter the rest of the bread crumb mixture over the top. Dot with the remaining butter and season with more pepper.
7 Bake in the oven for 20-30 minutes or until the top is crisp and brown. Serve at once.

Cook's Notes

TIME
Preparation takes 10 minutes, cooking 20-30 minutes.

SERVING IDEAS
Although cucumber is so often used raw, sliced in salads or sandwiches, there are many exciting ways in which it can be served hot, as an accompanying vegetable or in a sauce. Cucumber crisp is very good served with baked white fish steaks or fillets, roast chicken or broiled pork chops.

●115 calories per portion

Cucumber in wine vinegar

MAKES ABOUT 3-3½ LB
2 large cucumbers, total weight about 2 lb, scored and thinly sliced (see Preparation)
2 onions, thinly sliced in rings
3 tablespoons salt
2½ cups white wine vinegar
¾ cup sugar
1 teaspoon mustard seeds
1 teaspoon coriander seeds

1 Layer the cucumbers and onions in a large bowl, sprinkling each layer with salt. Cover and set aside for 2 hours. !

2 Meanwhile, select jars with vinegar-proof lids and sterilize them: Wash and thoroughly rinse the jars, then stand them on a rack in a large pan of water and bring to a boil. Remove the jars from the pan, stand upside-down to drain, then put them in a warm oven to dry out thoroughly.

3 Turn the vegetables out into a colander and rinse well in cold running water to remove the salt. Pat dry on absorbent kitchen paper, then spoon the vegetables into the jars, taking care not to pack them in too tightly.

4 Pour vinegar into an enameled or stainless steel saucepan. Add the sugar and seeds. Bring mixture to a boil, stirring until the sugar has dissolved, then lower the heat slightly and simmer gently for about 2 minutes.

5 Pour the hot vinegar over the vegetables in the jars, to cover completely, then seal tightly with the vinegar-proof lids. ! Label and store for at least 2 months before using.

Cook's Notes

TIME
Preparing and cooking the spiced vinegar mixture take 30 minutes, but allow 2 hours for salting. Store for 2 months before using.

WATCHPOINTS
Do not be tempted to cut the salting process; it is essential to draw out as much water as possible from the cucumber, otherwise the vinegar will be diluted.
Do not use jam pot covers to seal jars. They are not suitable as the vinegar may evaporate, allowing the pickle to shrink and dry out.

PREPARATION
For an attractive finish to the cucumber:

Score along the length of the whole cucumber with a fluting knife or a fork to remove long thin strips of peel. When sliced, the cucumber will have a fluted edge.

●25 calories per 1 oz

Curly kale with orange butter

SERVES 4
4½ cups shredded curly kale
¼ cup butter, softened
finely grated rind of ½ orange
1 tablespoon orange juice
**1 tablespoon soft brown bread
  crumbs**
**salt and freshly ground black
  pepper**

1 Beat the butter in a bowl with the orange rind, orange juice and bread crumbs. Season with salt and pepper to taste. Put on a piece of waxed paper and shape into a pat. Place in the freezer or freezing compartment of the refrigerator until required.
2 Bring a little salted water to a boil in a pan, add kale and return to a boil. Lower the heat, cover and simmer gently for 6-8 minutes, or until the kale is tender but still firm (see Cook's tip).

3 Drain well, then transfer the kale to a warmed serving dish.
4 Cut the butter into small pieces, place on top of the kale and toss well. Serve at once.

Cook's Notes

 TIME
Preparation takes about 10 minutes and cooking about 10 minutes.

COOK'S TIP
Use a steamer if you have one – steaming is an excellent way to cook kale because it prevents overcooking and soggy results. Put the shredded kale into the steamer and stand the steamer in a saucepan. Pour in boiling water to come just to the base of the steamer and set the pan over moderate heat so that the water is gently boiling. Cover and steam the kale for 10-12 minutes until tender.

 DID YOU KNOW
Kale, or curly kale as it is sometimes called, is a member of the cabbage family. It has tightly curled leaves. If unobtainable use finely shredded Savoy cabbage.

●120 calories per portion

Eggplant crisps with dip

SERVES 6
2 eggplants
vegetable oil, for sautéing

BATTER
2 cups all-purpose flour
1 teaspoon baking powder
generous pinch of salt
**generous sprinkling of freshly
    ground black pepper**
⅞ cup hot water
⅔ cup malt vinegar

DIP
⅔ cup sour cream
2 tablespoons chopped chives

1 Make the batter: Sift the flour, baking powder, salt and pepper into a large bowl. Make a well in the center and add the water. Using a whisk, gradually draw the flour into the liquid, then whisk in vinegar. Let stand for 30 minutes.

2 Meanwhile, halve the eggplants lengthwise, then cut into long slices, about ½ inch thick. Cut across the eggplant slices to make 2 inch sticks.

3 Spread the sticks out on a large plate, sprinkle with salt and let stand for 30 minutes.

4 Meanwhile, make the dip: Put the sour cream into a small serving bowl and mix in the chives. Season to taste with salt and pepper, cover and refrigerate until required.

5 Rinse the eggplants under cold running water, then pat them dry thoroughly with absorbent kitchen paper.

6 Preheat the oven to 225°.

7 Heat the oil in a deep-fat fryer to 350° or until a dry bread cube browns in 60 seconds.

8 Piercing with a fork, dip each stick into the batter, one at a time, to coat well. Fry a batch of coated sticks in the oil for about 5 minutes until golden brown. Remove with a slotted spoon and drain on absorbent kitchen paper. Keep warm in the oven; cook rest in same way.

9 Arrange the sticks on a warmed serving platter and serve them at once, with dip.

Cook's Notes

TIME
1 hour to make, including standing time.

SERVING IDEAS
These delicious sticks are ideal for serving with cocktails, or they make an excellent appetizer when you are serving a vegetarian meal.

●320 calories per portion

Eggplant savory

SERVES 4

1 lb eggplant, cut in ¼ inch slices
salt
2 tablespoons olive oil (see
Economy)
½ lb sliced bacon, rind removed
and diced
½ cup grated Parmesan cheese (see
Economy)
⅔ cup milk
freshly ground black pepper
2 tablespoons chopped parsley, for
garnish
margarine, for greasing

1 Put the eggplant slices in a single layer on a board or working surface and sprinkle evenly with 1 tablespoon salt. Let stand 30 minutes to remove the bitter juices.

2 Preheat the oven to 375° and grease an ovenproof dish.
3 Rinse the eggplant slices under cold running water, pat dry with absorbent kitchen paper and set aside.
4 Heat the oil in a large skillet, add the eggplant slices and sauté over moderate heat, turning once, until golden on both sides. Drain on absorbent kitchen paper.
5 Put the bacon in the skillet and cook it gently until lightly browned. Drain the bacon on absorbent kitchen paper.
6 Arrange a layer of eggplant in the base of the prepared dish, then a layer of bacon and a layer of cheese. Repeat twice, so that you have 3 layers of each. Season the milk well with salt and pepper and pour it over the top.
7 Bake in the oven for 35-40 minutes, until the top is golden.
8 Serve hot, sprinkled with the chopped parsley.

Cook's Notes

 TIME
Preparation takes about 25 minutes. Allow a further 30 minutes for salting and draining the eggplant. Cooking in the oven takes 35-40 minutes.

 ECONOMY
A cheaper vegetable oil may be used instead of olive oil, and Cheddar cheese instead of Parmesan.

 VARIATION
Zucchini may be used instead of eggplant.

 SERVING IDEAS
This substantial dish is really a meal in itself.

● 365 calories per portion

Eggplants on waffles

SERVES 4
2 large eggplants, cut in cubes
salt
2 tablespoons vegetable oil
1¼ cups beef broth
4 teaspoons tomato paste
2 cloves garlic, minced (optional)
½ teaspoon soft brown sugar
freshly ground black pepper
4 potato waffles
¾ cup shredded Cheddar cheese
coriander sprigs or parsley, for
   garnish

1 Layer the eggplant cubes in a colander, sprinkling each layer with salt. Put a plate on top and weight down. Leave to drain for about 30 minutes to remove the bitter juices. Rinse under cold running water, pat dry with absorbent kitchen paper or a clean dish towel.

2 Heat the oil in a large skillet, add the eggplant, broth, tomato paste, garlic, if using, and sugar. Season with salt and pepper.

3 Bring to a boil, then lower the heat, cover the pan and simmer for 8-10 minutes, stirring frequently, until the liquid is absorbed and the eggplant is tender.

4 Meanwhile, heat the broiler to high and toast the waffles for 4 minutes on each side or cook as directed on the package.

5 Place the waffles in a flameproof dish, pile the eggplant mixture on top and sprinkle over the grated cheese. Broil for 1-2 minutes (see Cook's tip).

6 Garnish waffles with coriander sprigs or parsley and serve at once.

Cook's Notes

TIME
Preparation and cooking take about 55-60 minutes, including salting the eggplant cubes.

SERVING IDEAS
This dish makes a light lunch or snack; for a more substantial meal double the quantities and serve 2 waffles per person.

COOK'S TIP
The cheese can be sprinkled on top of the eggplant and allowed to melt just before serving, without broiling, if preferred.

●295 calories per portion

Fennel with cheese

SERVES 4
2 fennel bulbs (total weight 1½ lb),
thinly sliced (see Preparation)
salt
2 tablespoons butter
4 tablespoons all-purpose flour
1 cup milk
1½ cups finely shredded Gruyère
or Cheddar cheese
¼ teaspoon freshly grated nutmeg
freshly ground black pepper
½ cup grated Parmesan cheese
margarine, for greasing

1 Heat the oven to 350°. Grease an ovenproof dish.
2 Bring a saucepan of salted water to a boil, add the fennel, bring back to a boil and cook for 6 minutes or until just tender.
3 Meanwhile, melt the butter in a saucepan, sprinkle in the flour and stir over low heat for 1-2 minutes until straw-colored. Remove from the heat and gradually stir in the milk. Return to the heat and simmer, stirring, until thick and smooth. Add shredded Gruyère and nutmeg and season to taste with salt and pepper. Stir well until the cheese is melted.
4 Drain the cooked fennel well, then stir into the cheese sauce. Transfer the fennel to the prepared dish and sprinkle with Parmesan cheese. ✳
5 Bake in the oven for 15 minutes until the topping is golden. Serve at once.

Cook's Notes

 TIME
Preparation 10 minutes; cooking 30 minutes.

 SERVING IDEAS
Serve as a vegetarian main dish accompanied by sautéed potatoes and a mixed salad. Alternatively, serve with white meat.

 FREEZING
This dish can be frozen before baking: Make in a foil container, cover with the lid, then seal, label and freeze for up to 3 months. To serve: Bake from frozen in uncovered foil container in a 375° oven for 30 minutes.

 PREPARATION
To slice a bulb of fennel thinly:

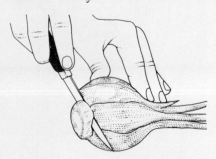

Trim away bulb base and all wispy leaves. Using a long, sharp knife, cut through the fennel bulb vertically.

● 375 calories per portion

Jerusalem artichoke soup

SERVES 4-6
2 lb Jerusalem artichokes (see Preparation)
1 tablespoon margarine or butter
2 onions, chopped
2½ cups milk
1¾ cups chicken broth
salt and freshly ground black pepper
chopped fresh parsley

1 Melt the margarine in a large saucepan, add the onions and sauté gently for 5 minutes until soft and lightly colored.
2 Add the artichokes to the pan, together with the milk, broth and salt and pepper to taste.
3 Bring to a boil, ! lower the heat slightly, cover and simmer for about 30 minutes, until the artichokes are soft.
4 Let cool slightly, then work in a blender or food processor until smooth. Or work mixture through a vegetable mill.
5 Return the soup to the rinsed-out pan and reheat gently. Taste and adjust seasoning, then pour into warmed individual soup bowls. Serve at once, garnished with chopped parsley.

Cook's Notes

 TIME
15 minutes preparation, 30 minutes cooking

 WATCHPOINT
Keep an eye on the soup as it is coming to a boil, since the milk content will make it boil over very quickly.

 PREPARATION
Artichokes are tricky to peel but if you parboil them first, it is much easier.
If preferred, leave the skins on and scrub before cooking. They give a nutty flavor.

 PRESSURE COOKING
Bring to high (H) pressure and cook for 10 minutes only, without the milk. Heat the milk separately and add to blender while puréeing.

 SERVING IDEAS
Serve with croutons and a swirl of cream.

●175 calories per portion

Kohlrabi and watercress soup

SERVES 4-6

1 bunch watercress
1 lb kohlrabi or turnips, diced (see Did you know)
2 tablespoons margarine or butter
2 bacon slices, rind removed and chopped
1 onion, chopped
4 cups chicken broth
salt and freshly ground black pepper
⅔ cup light cream, to finish

1 Melt the margarine in a large saucepan, add the chopped bacon and onion and sauté gently for 5 minutes until the onion is soft and lightly colored.
2 Add the diced kohlrabi and sauté gently, stirring, for 5 minutes.
3 Pour in the chicken broth and bring to a boil. Lower the heat slightly, cover the pan and simmer for about 45 minutes until the kohlrabi are soft.
4 Reserve a few sprigs of watercress for garnish and add the rest to the soup. Bring back to a boil, then lower the heat slightly and simmer for 2 minutes.
5 Remove the pan from the heat and press soup through a strainer, or let cool slightly, then purée in a blender. Return the soup to the rinsed-out pan and heat through until bubbling.
6 Taste and adjust seasoning then pour into warmed individual soup bowls. Swirl cream into each portion and garnish with the reserved watercress sprigs. Serve the soup at once.

Cook's Notes

 TIME
10 minutes preparation, 1 hour cooking.

 DID YOU KNOW
The purple-skinned kohlrabi is believed to have originated in the East. It has a turnip-like flavor and is prepared and worked in the same way.

● 190 calories per portion

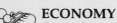 **ECONOMY**
Omit the cream, or substitute half-and-half. The bacon may also be omitted, but the flavor of the finished soup will be milder.

 SERVING IDEAS
This soup may be served chilled, as well as hot. When serving chilled, allow it to cool then swirl plain yogurt into the soup.

Leek and tomato casserole

SERVES 4-6
2 large leeks, trimmed, washed and cut in 1 inch pieces (see Preparation)
2 large onions, cut in eighths
14 oz can tomatoes
1 tablespoon finely chopped parsley
1 bay leaf
2 cloves garlic, minced (optional)
1 teaspoon salt
freshly ground black pepper
⅔ cup chicken or vegetable broth
¼ cup vegetable oil
1 tablespoon lemon juice
pinch of dried thyme

1 Preheat the oven to 350°.
2 Put all the ingredients into a large bowl and mix well. Turn into a large ovenproof dish or casserole, cover and cook in the oven for 1½-2 hours, until tender. Serve hot.

Cook's Notes

 TIME
Preparation of vegetables takes 15 minutes; cooking time in the oven is 1½-2 hours.

 ECONOMY
Save fuel by cooking this dish with a roast, on the shelf below the meat.

 SERVING IDEAS
Serve this easy-to-make vegetable dish with beef, pork or lamb roast.

 VARIATION
When tomatoes are cheap and plentiful, use fresh instead of canned, in which case you may need a little extra broth. Peel them before mixing with other ingredients.

 PREPARATION
Trim leeks; slit them down almost to base. Fan out under cold running water to rinse off all dirt.

● 175 calories per portion

Leeks Chinese-style

SERVES 4-6
½ lb leeks, cut in 2 inch lengths
   (see Preparation)
2 tablespoons margarine
1 onion, sliced
½ cup cup walnut pieces
4 celery stalks, chopped
½ lb stem lettuce, sliced (see
   Buying guide)
salt and freshly ground black pepper
a few dashes of soy sauce

1 Melt the margarine in a skillet, add the leeks and onion and sauté gently for 5 minutes (see Cook's tip) until the onion is soft and lightly colored.
2 Add the walnuts, together with the celery, and sauté over moderate heat, stirring, for 3 minutes.
3 Stir the stem lettuce into the pan and cook for a further 2 minutes until the stem lettuce begins to soften.
4 Season to taste with salt and pepper, stir in a few dashes of soy sauce and cook for a further minute. Turn into a warmed serving dish and serve at once.

Cook's Notes

 TIME
Preparation and cooking take about 30 minutes.

 PREPARATION
Trim the leeks, then slit them down the center almost to the base. Fan out under cold running water to rinse off all the dirt.

 BUYING GUIDE
Stem lettuce or celtuce is very economical, needing almost no trimming.

 VARIATIONS
Omit the walnuts and add tomato paste or canned chopped tomatoes and a little oregano instead.

To make the dish more substantial, pour cheese sauce over the top, sprinkle with bread crumbs, dot with butter and bake in a 425° oven until the top is crisp.

Green onions make a very good substitute for the leeks: Cook them in the same way.

 COOK'S TIP
If you prefer leeks slightly less crunchy, cover the pan during the first 5 minutes of cooking.

●170 calories per portion

Lettuce in cheese sauce

SERVES 4
1 large head crisp-hearted lettuce (see Buying guide)
salt
2 tablespoons butter
¼ cup chicken broth

CHEESE SAUCE
2 tablespoons margarine or butter
¼ cup all-purpose flour
1¼ cups milk
½ cup shredded Cheddar cheese
¼ teaspoon prepared English mustard
freshly ground black pepper
1 tablespoon grated Parmesan cheese

1 Preheat the oven to 350°.
2 Discard the outer lettuce leaves if coarse or damaged, but leave the lettuce whole. Bring a saucepan of salted water to a boil and put the lettuce in it to blanch for 5 minutes. Drain well.
3 Cut the blanched lettuce into quarters and place in a shallow flameproof dish. Dot with the butter and pour the broth around the lettuce in the dish. Cook in the oven for 30 minutes or until the lettuce is tender.
4 Meanwhile, make the sauce: Melt the margarine in a small saucepan, sprinkle in the flour and stir over low heat for 1-2 minutes until straw-colored. Remove from the heat and gradually stir in the milk. Return to the heat and simmer, stirring, until the sauce is thick and smooth.
5 Off heat, stir in the Cheddar cheese until melted. Stir in the mustard and season to taste with salt and pepper. Heat the broiler to high.
6 When the lettuce is cooked, drain well, reserving 2 tablespoons of the cooking liquid. Return the cooked lettuce to the dish.
7 Stir the reserved cooking liquid into the cheese sauce.
8 Pour the cheese sauce evenly over the lettuce in the dish. Sprinkle the Parmesan cheese over the top and set under the broiler for a few minutes until the cheese has melted and the top is browned. Serve hot.

Cook's Notes

 TIME
Preparation takes about 15 minutes. Cooking the lettuce and making the sauce takes about 40 minutes.

 VARIATION
Use a small head of stem lettuce instead of regular lettuce and extend the cooking time if necessary.

 SERVING IDEAS
Serve with baked fish or chicken or pork roast.

 BUYING GUIDE
You need a really crisp, firm lettuce for this dish: Iceberg or Crisphead would be best, with their compact leaves.

●210 calories per portion

Mushrooms with garlic peas

SERVES 4
4 large or 8 medium flat mushrooms
¼ cup butter
2 cloves garlic, minced (optional)
2 tablespoons chopped parsley
salt and freshly ground black pepper
½ lb frozen peas, thawed
margarine, for greasing

1 Preheat the oven to 350°.
2 Remove the mushroom stems and chop them finely. Wipe the mushroom caps and put them, stem-sides up, in a well-greased ovenproof dish.
3 With a wooden spoon, mash the butter and mix in the chopped mushroom stems, garlic, if using, parsley and salt and pepper.

4 Divide the peas equally between the mushroom caps, spooning them on top. Dot with the flavored butter.

5 Cover the dish with foil and bake in the oven for 20 minutes until the mushrooms are tender. Serve at once, straight from the dish.

Cook's Notes

 TIME
Preparation 10 minutes, cooking 20 minutes. Allow 2 hours for thawing the peas.

SERVING IDEAS
This is an impressive way of serving mushrooms and peas for company or a dinner party because they can be arranged attractively around the edge of a serving platter – with a meat roast presented in the center.
They would go well with lamb (crown roast in particular).

 BUYING GUIDE
Make sure the mushrooms are really fresh when you buy them: The caps should be white and the stem sides pinkish-grey. Avoid any that look slimy or wrinkled.

 VARIATION
If you want to use fresh peas for this recipe, cook them for 5-10 minutes in boiling salted water first. For ½ lb shelled peas you will need about 1½ lb peas in the pod.

●120 calories per portion.

Mushrooms with nutmeg

SERVES 4
¾ lb button mushrooms (see
  Buying guide)
2 tablespoons margarine or butter
1 onion, minced
salt and freshly ground black pepper
freshly grated nutmeg
⅔ cup sour cream
½ teaspoon paprika

1 Melt the margarine in a large skillet, add the onion and sauté gently for 5 minutes until soft and lightly colored.
2 Add the whole mushrooms, stir well and cook gently for 3 minutes, until they begin to soften.
3 Season well with salt and pepper, and add grated nutmeg to taste.
4 Stir in the sour cream (see Cook's tip) and heat through for 1 minute over low heat.
5 Turn the mushroom mixture into a warmed serving dish, sprinkle with paprika and serve at once.

Cook's Notes

 TIME
5 minutes preparation, 10 minutes cooking.

 BUYING GUIDE
Buy small and even-size mushrooms, since they are kept whole in this dish.

 VARIATION
Substitute chopped chives for the paprika.

 COOK'S TIP
Always stir sour cream before adding it to hot food – this helps to make a smooth sauce.

 SERVING IDEAS
These deliciously creamy mushrooms make an excellent accompaniment to roast or broiled meat. Alternatively, serve them on toast as a snack.

●145 calories per portion

Okra Mediterranean-style

SERVES 4
1 lb okra (see Buying guide and
    Preparation)
¼ cup vegetable oil
1 large onion, chopped
1 lb tomatoes, peeled and
    quartered
1 clove garlic, minced,
1 teaspoon ground coriander
salt and freshly ground black pepper
coriander leaves, for garnish

1 Heat the oil in a large saucepan,
add onion and sauté for 5 minutes.
2 Add the okra to the pan, stir to
coat well with the oil, then add the
tomatoes, garlic and coriander. Stir
well to mix, then season to taste.
3 Bring to a boil, then lower the
heat slightly, cover and simmer for
30 minutes until okra is tender.
Serve garnished with coriander.

Cook's Notes

 TIME
Preparation and cook-
ing take about 40 minu-
tes in total.

 SERVING IDEAS
This dish is a natural
accompaniment to
broiled lamb chops or kabobs. It
is also delicious served with
either plain boiled or fried rice as
a main course.

BUYING GUIDE
Okra, one of the essen-
tial ingredients of Creole
cooking, is now widely available
all over America.

Canned okra is also obtainable
and may be used in this recipe,
but the flavor and texture will
not be so good.

● 165 calories per portion

 PREPARATION
To prepare the okra for
this dish:

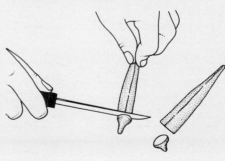

*Trim the okra and remove any
blemishes with a sharp knife. It is
not necessary to pare the okra before
they are cooked.*

 VARIATION
Replace the fresh toma-
toes with 14 oz can
tomatoes, but use only half the
canned juice, otherwise the dish
will be too watery.

Onion
and cheese ring

SERVES 4-6

1½ cups shredded Cheddar cheese
   (see Buying guide)
½ teaspoon mixed dried herbs
2 onions, finely chopped
1 tablespoon Dijon mustard
salt and freshly ground black pepper
13 oz frozen basic pie dough,
   thawed
1 small egg, beaten, to seal and
   glaze
1 teaspoon poppy seeds (optional)
margarine, for greasing
watercress, for garnish

1 Preheat the oven to 400°. Grease a baking sheet.
2 Mix the cheese, herbs, onions, and mustard together in a bowl and season to taste.
3 Roll out the dough on a floured surface to make a rectangle about 16 × 11 inches. Trim the edges so they are straight and neat.
4 Spread the cheese and onion mixture evenly over the dough, bringing it almost to the edge. Brush 1 long edge of the dough with beaten egg. Starting from the other long edge, roll up the dough like a jelly roll. Press along its length to seal.
5 Carefully place the roll seam-side down on the baking sheet and, using scissors, snip along one edge at 1 inch intervals, taking care not to cut right through. Shape the roll into a ring, brush one end with beaten egg and press the ends together, to seal securely.
6 Lift the base of each cut section and tilt slightly to the side, so that filling is exposed (see Preparation).
7 Brush the surface of the dough with beaten egg and sprinkle with poppy seeds, if using. Bake the ring in the oven for 30-35 minutes, until the pastry is golden. ⚠
8 Place the baking sheet on a wire rack and leave until cool enough to handle easily. Using 2 slotted spatulas, carefully lift onto a serving plate. Garnish with watercress.

Cook's Notes

TIME
Preparation takes 30 minutes and cooking 30-35 minutes. Allow about 10 minutes for the ring to cool slightly.

BUYING GUIDE
Choose the cheese that suits your taste. American Cheddars are now very good. They range in flavor from mild to sharp, and in color from cream to deep orange. Varieties to look for: Herkimer, Colby, Vermont, Wisconsin.

SERVING IDEAS
This rich cheesy ring is best eaten warm. Serve with green salad for lunch or thinly sliced with cocktails.

WATCHPOINT
Take care not to overcook the ring, as the dough browns very quickly.

PREPARATION
Two stages in forming cheese and onion ring:

1 The shaped ring is snipped at 1 inch intervals

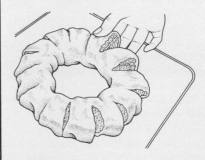

2 The cut sections are lifted and tilted at a slight angle

● 615 calories per portion

Onions with orange stuffing

SERVES 4

4 onions, weighing about 6 oz each
2 tablespoons margarine or butter
1 tablespoon chopped parsley
1 tablespoon chopped thyme or
** 1 teaspoon dried**
2 cups soft wholewheat bread
** crumbs**
grated rind and juice of 1 orange
2 teaspoons Dijon mustard
⅞ cup boiling chicken broth
parsley sprigs and lemon slices, for
** garnish**

1 Preheat the oven to 350°.
2 Peel the onions, removing both the outer skin and the thin transpa-rent inner skin. Cut a slice ½ inch thick from the top of each onion.
3 Using a teaspoon and a small sharp knife, remove the inside of the onions, leaving a shell about ¼ inch thick. Finely chop half the scooped-out onion. (Reserve the rest for use in another dish.)
4 Melt the margarine in a skillet, add the chopped onion and sauté gently for about 5 minutes until soft but not colored, stirring occa-sionally.
5 Remove the pan from the heat and mix in the herbs, bread crumbs, orange rind and juice and mustard.
6 Spoon the stuffing into the onion, packing it in tightly. Stand the onions in a casserole, then pour the boiling broth around them.
7 Cover and bake for 1 hour. Serve at once, garnished with pars-ley and lemon slices.

Cook's Notes

 TIME
Preparing the onions and the stuffing, 30 mi-nutes. Cooking, 1 hour.

 SERVING IDEAS
Serve with sausage links or cheesy dishes.

FREEZING
Stuffed onions freeze well. Cool after baking, then place side by side in a rigid container with the broth. Freeze for up to 6-8 weeks. Thaw by placing in a covered casserole in an oven preheated to 350° for 40 minutes.

●155 calories per portion

Onions with raisins

SERVES 4
1 lb pearl onions (see Buying guide and Preparation)
¼ cup olive oil
½ cup golden raisins
1¼ cups chicken broth
¼ cup wine vinegar
1 clove garlic, minced
1 tablespoon tomato paste
bouquet garni
salt and freshly ground black pepper
chopped parsley, for garnish

1 Place the onions in a large pan with the oil, raisins, broth, vinegar, garlic, tomato paste and bouquet garni. Season to taste with salt and pepper.
2 Bring the contents of the pan to a boil, then lower the heat, cover and simmer for 40-50 minutes until the onions are tender when pierced with a sharp knife.
3 Remove the bouquet garni and transfer to a serving dish. Serve hot or cold sprinkled with parsley.

Cook's Notes

 TIME
20 minutes preparation, and about 40-50 minutes cooking time.

 PREPARATION
Peeling small onions can be tedious. To make the task easier, plunge them first into boiling water, then immediately into cold water. The skins will then slide off quite easily.

 BUYING GUIDE
It is best to buy the tiny pearl onions, but you can use larger ones.

 SERVING IDEAS
These tiny onions are equally good hot or cold. Serve them with hot French bread for an appetizer or snack.

●215 calories per portion

Parsnip and nutmeg croquettes

SERVES 4-6
1½ lb parsnips, cut in 1 inch
   chunks
salt
½ cup butter, diced
1 tablespoon milk
¼ teaspoon freshly grated nutmeg
1 tablespoon chopped fresh parsley
1 small egg, lightly beaten
freshly ground black pepper
¾ cup dried white bread crumbs
all-purpose flour, for rolling
vegetable oil, for deep frying
parsley sprigs, for garnish.

1 Bring the parsnips to a boil in salted water, lower the heat and cook for 20 minutes or until they are very tender.

2 Drain parsnips well and then return to the pan (see Cook's tip). Add the butter and milk and mash until smooth. Stir in the nutmeg, parsley and egg, then season to taste with pepper. Turn the mixture into a bowl, cover and let cool completely for about 1 hour.

3 Preheat the oven to 225°.

4 Spread the bread crumbs out on a plate. With floured hands, divide the parsnip mixture into about 20 equal-size pieces; roll each piece into a ball. Roll the balls in the plate of bread crumbs to coat each one thoroughly.

5 Heat the oil in a deep-fat fryer to 375° or until a dry bread cube browns in 50 seconds.

6 Fry a few of the croquettes for 4-5 minutes until golden brown. Drain on absorbent kitchen paper and keep hot in the oven while frying the remaining batches of parsnip croquettes. ⚠

7 Garnish the parsnip and nutmeg croquettes with parsley and serve.

Cook's Notes

 TIME
30 minutes preparation, plus 1 hour cooling. Frying takes about 20 minutes.

 SERVING IDEAS
Parsnip and nutmeg croquettes are rather sweet and nutty tasting. Serve them around a meat roast, or alternatively as an accompaniment to broiled chicken or pork chops.

If preferred, try serving them as a tasty vegetarian meal, topped with shredded Cheddar cheese or a homemade tomato sauce – accompany with small bowls of watercress sprigs and cucumber wedges, garnished with chopped hard-cooked egg.

 COOK'S TIP
Stir the parsnips over low heat for 1 minute to make sure that they are completely dry, otherwise the mix will be too mushy to shape.

●395 calories per portion

 DID YOU KNOW
Nutmeg was a very popular spice in 17th century England, so much so that travellers often carried a small pocket grater around so they could have freshly grated nutmeg on their food and their drinks.

WATCHPOINT
Remember to reheat the vegetable oil between frying the separate batches of croquettes.

Pea soufflé

SERVES 4

½ lb peas, unshelled weight,
   shelled (see Buying guide)
salt
1 tablespoon vegetable oil
1 cup finely chopped button
   mushrooms
4 teaspoons minced onion
2 tablespoons butter
¼ cup all-purpose flour
⅔ cup milk
4 large eggs, separated
pinch of freshly grated nutmeg
freshly ground black pepper
margarine, for greasing

1 Bring a pan of salted water to a boil, add the peas, lower the heat and simmer for about 20 minutes until quite tender. Drain well, then press through a sieve or purée in a blender.

2 Preheat the oven to 400° (see Cook's tip). Grease a 5-cup soufflé mold with margarine.

3 Heat the oil in a skillet, add the mushrooms and onion and sauté gently for 5 minutes until soft and lightly colored. Set aside.

4 Melt the butter in a saucepan, sprinkle in the flour and stir over low heat for 1-2 minutes until straw-colored. Off heat, gradually stir in the milk. Return to heat and simmer, stirring, until thick and smooth. Stir in the pea purée and remove the pan from the heat.

5 Add the egg yolks, one at a time, beating well after each addition. Season with nutmeg and salt and pepper to taste.

6 In a clean, dry bowl, beat the egg whites until they stand in stiff peaks. Fold into pea mixture with a metal spoon.

7 Add 2 tablespoons of pea mixture to mushrooms and fold in lightly.

8 Spoon half the pea mixture (without mushrooms) into the greased soufflé mold. Spoon the mushroom mixture into a mound in the center. ⚠ Cover with remaining pea mixture.

9 Bake in the oven for about 40 minutes or until the soufflé is well risen and golden. Serve the soufflé at once, straight from the mold.

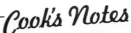

Cook's Notes

 TIME
50 minutes preparation; 40 minutes cooking.

 BUYING GUIDE
This amount of fresh peas in their pods will yield about ½ lb shelled peas. Alternatively, use ½ lb frozen peas, but boil for only 8 minutes in stage 1.

 COOK'S TIP
For the best results, preheat a baking sheet on shelf on which the soufflé is to be cooked. The extra heat from the sheet, at the base of the soufflé, helps the cooking and rising.

 WATCHPOINT
Add the mushroom mixture gently – the mushrooms will sink but will keep together to form a surprise center in the soufflé.

SERVING IDEAS
This soufflé is ideal as a light lunch dish, served with a salad of garden cress, endive and orange in a sharp oil and vinegar dressing.

 DID YOU KNOW
In French cooking, the name *Saint Germain* implies that peas are included.

●260 calories per portion

Peas in basil butter

SERVES 4

1 lb snow peas, trimmed (see Buying guide)
salt
¼ cup butter, softened
1 teaspoon dried basil (see Buying guide)
½ teaspoon grated orange rind
freshly ground black pepper
2 orange twists, for garnish

1 Bring a pan of salted water to a boil, add the peas and bring back to a boil. Lower the heat, cover and simmer for 5 minutes until just tender, but still crisp. ⚠
2 Meanwhile, beat the butter in a small bowl with the basil, orange rind and a little pepper. Mix until well blended.
3 Drain the pods thoroughly in a colander, ⚠ then return to the pan. Add the butter mixture and toss gently over low heat until the pods are thoroughly coated.
4 Turn the peas into a warmed serving dish, garnish with orange twists and serve at once.

Cook's Notes

TIME
Preparation and cooking of the snow peas take about 15 minutes.

BUYING GUIDE
Choose bright, crisp pods that have no yellow markings. Avoid very large pods, they will be past their best and rather tough.
  If fresh basil is available, use 2 teaspoons in place of the dried basil.

! WATCHPOINTS
Take care not to overcook the peas or they will lose some of their texture and color.
  Make sure that the peas are very well drained before tossing them in butter.

● 105 calories per portion

Peas and pears in tarragon

SERVES 4
¾ lb frozen peas
¾ lb ripe, but firm pears (see Buying guide)
salt
2 tablespoons butter
1-2 teaspoons dried tarragon (see Watchpoint)
freshly ground black pepper
sprigs of tarragon, for garnish

1 Bring a small quantity of salted water to a boil and cook the peas according to package directions.
2 Meanwhile, peel and core the pears and cut them in chunks. Melt the butter over very gentle heat, add the pears and sauté gently for about 5 minutes until soft but not mushy. Stir in the tarragon.
3 Drain the peas and add them to the pan, season to taste with pepper, then gently mix together.
4 Turn the peas and pears into a warmed serving dish, scraping the pan to ensure the juices are added. Garnish with tarragon and serve.

Cook's Notes

 TIME
This dish takes about 5 minutes to prepare and about 8 minutes to cook.

WATCHPOINT
Tarragon has quite an unusual, distinctive aniseed flavor. If you are not familiar with the taste, and are not sure how much to add, use just 1 teaspoon of dried tarragon the very first time you try this recipe.

 SERVING IDEAS
The light and delicate flavor of this dish makes it a particularly good vegetable accompaniment to broiled fish or roast chicken.

BUYING GUIDE
Choose pears that are ripe rather than very hard – Bartletts have the best flavor for this recipe.

●120 calories per portion

Peas with water chestnuts

SERVES 4
½ lb snow peas (see Buying guide)
2 tablespoons vegetable oil
4 scallions, cut in 2 inch lengths
8 oz can water chestnuts, drained
   and sliced
2 tablespoons soy sauce
½ teaspoon sugar
¼ cup chicken broth
salt and freshly ground black
   pepper

1 Trim the snow peas and, if necessary, remove any strings from the pod sides.
2 Heat the oil in a wok or a large skillet, add the scallions, snow peas and water chestnuts and stir until the vegetables are thoroughly coated with oil.
3 Add the soy sauce, sugar and chicken broth and stir-fry over moderate heat for about 5 minutes, stirring constantly, until the vegetables are hot but still crisp.
4 Season stir-fried vegetables to taste with salt and pepper, then turn into a warmed serving dish and serve at once.

Cook's Notes

 TIME
15 minutes preparation and cooking.

 SERVING IDEAS
Serve this as part of a Chinese meal with a beef dish or crispy roast duck.

 BUYING GUIDE
Snow peas tend to be quite expensive, but are well worth buying occasionally for their delicate flavor.
  If fresh snow peas are not available, buy them frozen from supermarket deep freezers.

 VARIATION
Use 1 cup sliced mushrooms instead of the water chestnuts.

●100 calories per portion

Pepper kabobs

SERVES 6
1 green and 1 sweet red pepper,
  each seeded and cut in about
  12 squares
12 pearl onions
salt
12 button mushrooms
1 lb can pineapple cubes, drained
vegetable oil, for greasing

SAUCE
1¼ cups plain yogurt
2 cloves garlic, minced
2 inch piece of fresh gingerroot,
  pared and grated
2 teaspoons garam masala
juice of 1 lemon
pinch of salt

1 Make the sauce: Put all the sauce ingredients in a bowl, mix well and leave to stand for 30 minutes to allow the flavors to blend.

2 Meanwhile, blanch the peppers and onions: Bring a large pan of salted water to a boil, add the peppers and onions and boil for 1 minute. Drain and immediately plunge into cold water to prevent further cooking. Drain well again and pat dry with absorbent kitchen paper.

3 Preheat the broiler to moderate.

4 Divide the peppers, onions, mushrooms and pineapple pieces into 6 portions and thread them onto 6 oiled metal kabob skewers, alternating the shapes and colors as much as possible.

5 Lay the skewers on a baking sheet or broiler pan and brush with some of the sauce. Broil the kabobs for about 8 minutes, turning them every few minutes and brushing with more sauce, until vegetables are evenly browned. Serve at once.

Cook's Notes

TIME
1 hour to prepare and cook the spicy vegetable kabobs from start to finish.

SERVING IDEAS
These kabobs make an excellent vegetarian dish, served with lightly spiced brown and white rice.
   Alternatively, the kabobs are ideal for cookouts on a barbecue, and make especially good accompaniments to grilled chops and burgers.

VARIATION
Try adding bacon rolls to each skewer for more substantial kabobs. Use three bacon rolls per skewer.

● 100 calories per portion

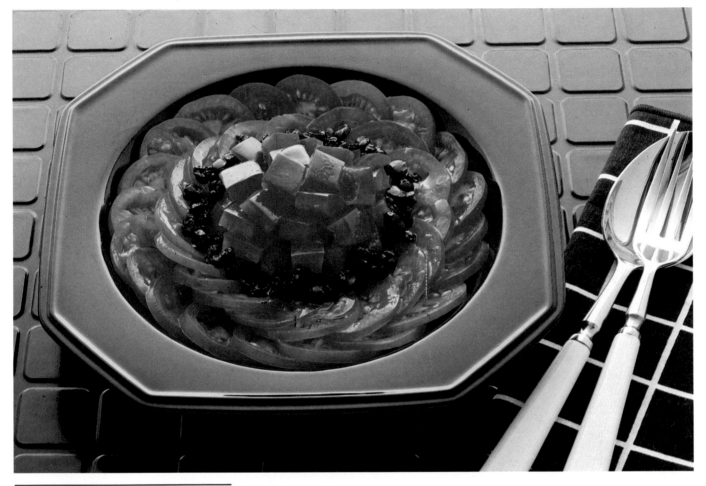

Pepper and tomato salad

SERVES 4
1 lb tomatoes (see Buying guide)
1 large sweet red pepper
⅓ cup dried currants

DRESSING
¼ cup olive oil (see Economy)
2 tablespoons white wine vinegar
¼ teaspoon hot pepper sauce
1 clove garlic, minced with a pinch of salt (optional)

1 Slice the tomatoes thinly (see Preparation) and arrange them on a serving plate so that they form overlapping circles.
2 Seed and dice the pepper and pile it on top of the tomatoes, in the center of the serving plate.
3 Scatter the currants in a ring round the diced peppers.
4 Beat the ingredients for the dressing together until well blended and spoon evenly over the salad. ⚠ Serve at once.

Cook's Notes

 TIME
The salad takes 20 minutes to prepare.

 WATCHPOINT
Do not dress the salad until just before serving, or the tomatoes may become soggy.

 ECONOMY
Although the flavor of olive oil is perfect for tomatoes, sunflower oil makes an acceptable substitute, and is considerably cheaper.

 SERVING IDEAS
This sweet colorful salad goes well with cheese and egg dishes.

 PREPARATION
Use a knife with a serrated edge to cut the tomatoes into thin, even slices.

 BUYING GUIDE
Choose firm, sweet, even-size tomatoes for best results.

● 70 calories per portion

Peppers with sunflower seeds

SERVES 4

2 green peppers, halved lengthwise and seeded (see Buying guide)
2 tablespoons sunflower or vegetable oil
1 large onion, chopped
1 sweet red pepper, seeded and cut in ½ inch squares
1 lb tomatoes, peeled and chopped
1 cup quartered button mushrooms
¼ cup sunflower seeds, toasted (see Buying guide and Preparation)
½ teaspoon dried thyme
¼ teaspoon paprika
salt and freshly ground black pepper
⅓ cup coarsely shredded Edam or Gouda cheese
4 ripe olives (optional)

1 Heat the oil in a medium saucepan, add the onion and sauté gently for 5 minutes until soft and lightly colored. Add the red pepper and cook for a further 2 minutes, stirring. Add the tomatoes, mushrooms, toasted sunflower seeds, thyme, paprika and salt and pepper to taste, then cook over a moderate heat for 10 minutes, stirring until the mixture is thick.

2 Meanwhile, bring a saucepan of salted water to a boil. Put in the green pepper halves, bring back to a boil, lower heat and simmer for 6 minutes, until just tender. Drain.

3 Heat the broiler to high. Put the green pepper halves on the broiler rack and season them inside with salt and pepper. Pile the sunflower seed mixture into the pepper halves, pressing it down with a spoon. Sprinkle the cheese lightly on top; garnish with olives, if liked.

4 Broil for a few minutes, until the cheese is melted but not brown. Serve at once.

Cook's Notes

 TIME
Preparation and broiling take about 35 minutes.

BUYING GUIDE
Buy 2 fairly large, fat green peppers, so that there is room for the filling.
Sunflower seeds are available from good supermarkets and delicatessens and from health food stores.

PREPARATION
To toast the sunflower seeds, sprinkle them in a layer cake pan and toast under a hot broiler until golden, shaking the pan frequently so that the seeds brown evenly. Do not let them get too brown or the flavor will be spoiled.

●215 calories per portion

Potato gnocchi and tomato sauce

SERVES 4
1½ lb potatoes
1 cup all-purpose flour
2 tablespoons butter, softened
pinch of freshly grated nutmeg
1 egg yolk, beaten
½ cup grated Parmesan cheese
margarine or butter, for greasing

TOMATO SAUCE
1 small onion, minced
1 clove garlic, minced
5 oz can tomato paste
1½ cups water
1 teaspoon sugar
1 bay leaf
pinch of dried basil
salt and freshly ground black pepper

1 Make the sauce first: Place all the ingredients in a pan with salt and pepper to taste. Bring to a boil, then lower the heat, cover and simmer gently for 30 minutes.

2 Meanwhile, bring the potatoes to a boil in salted water, lower the heat and cook for 20 minutes until fork-tender. Drain, then pass through a strainer into a bowl.

3 Work the sauce through a pot strainer then return to the rinsed-out pan. Set aside. Grease an oven-proof dish and heat oven to 225°.

4 Beat the flour into the potatoes with the butter, nutmeg and salt and pepper to taste. Add just enough of the beaten egg yolk to bind the mixture. Work in ⅓ cup of the grated Parmesan.

5 Bring a large pan of lightly salted water to a simmer.

6 Meanwhile, turn the potato mixture onto a floured surface, divide into 3 and form each piece into a roll about 1 inch in diameter. Cut each roll into 1 inch slices.

7 Drop slices from 1 roll into the simmering water. Cook for about 5 minutes, or until they rise to the surface and look puffy. Remove with a slotted spoon, place in the prepared dish and keep hot in the oven while you cook the remaining pieces in the same way.

8 Reheat the tomato sauce. Preheat the broiler to high.

9 Pour a little of the warmed tomato sauce over the gnocchi and top with the remaining Parmesan. Place under the broiler for about 5 min-utes until the top is golden and bubbling. Serve the gnocchi at once, straight from the dish, with the remaining sauce passed separately in a warmed sauceboat.

Cook's Notes

 TIME
The cooking and pre-paration should take about 1¼ hours, plus 30 minutes for chilling.

SERVING IDEAS
Serve for supper follow-ed by a green salad.

 WATCHPOINT
Be careful not to make the mixture too wet. Then, to help shape it easily, refrigerate for 30 minutes.

DID YOU KNOW
Gnocchi is the Italian word for dumplings. They are most commonly made using semolina flour.

●380 calories per portion

Potatoes paprika

SERVES 4
1½ lb potatoes
salt
2 tablespoons vegetable oil
1 medium onion, sliced
1 teaspoon paprika
1¼ cups chicken broth
½ teaspoon caraway seeds
(optional)
1 large tomato, peeled and chopped
freshly ground black pepper
3 tablespoons sour cream
extra paprika, for garnish

1 Boil the potatoes in salted water until they are beginning to soften – about 7 minutes. Drain and cut in ¼ inch slices.

2 Heat the oil in a large saucepan and sauté the onion over moderate heat for about 4 minutes, or until it is just beginning to turn light brown. Add the paprika, chicken broth, caraway seeds, if using, tomato and pepper. Stir well to mix, then add the potatoes, stirring carefully.

3 Bring slowly to a boil, cover the pan and simmer for 20-25 minutes. The potatoes should have absorbed most of the liquid.

4 Pour over the sour cream and allow just to heat through. Turn onto a warmed serving dish. Sprinkle with a little extra paprika for garnish.

Cook's Notes

 TIME
This tasty dish takes 45 minutes to make.

 DID YOU KNOW
Caraway seeds have an aniseed taste which imparts a very definite flavor to food.

●265 calories per portion

Pumpkin soup

SERVES 6
2 lb pumpkin, seeded and cut in
  1 inch cubes (see Variation)
salt
3 tablespoons butter
1 large onion, finely chopped
2 tomatoes, peeled and chopped
1 teaspoon chopped chives
¼ teaspoon freshly grated nutmeg
1 tablespoon shredded coconut
2½ cups chicken broth
freshly ground black pepper
1¼ cups light cream
paprika, for garnish

1 Put the pumpkin into a saucepan, add enough water just to cover and a good pinch of salt. Bring to a boil, then lower the heat slightly and simmer for 15 minutes. Drain well.
2 Melt the butter in a saucepan, add the onion and sauté gently for 5 minutes until soft and lightly colored.
3 Add the pumpkin, tomatoes, chives, nutmeg and coconut and cook gently for a further 5 minutes.
4 Pour in the broth, season with salt and pepper to taste and bring to a boil. Lower the heat slightly, cover and simmer the mixture for about 30 minutes.
5 Remove the pan from the heat, let cool slightly, then purée in a blender. Stir in half the cream.
6 Pour the soup into warmed soup bowls, then swirl in the remaining cream and sprinkle with paprika. Serve at once.

Cook's Notes

TIME
10 minutes preparation, 55 minutes cooking, including simmering pumpkin.

 FREEZING
Pour the purée into a rigid container, leaving headspace. Cool quickly, then seal, label and freeze for up to 3 months. To serve: Thaw at room temperature for about 4 hours, then heat through and add the cream and paprika.

VARIATION
If you are unable to buy pumpkin, carrots are a very good substitute and they do not need precooking.

 SERVING IDEAS
This soup is good either hot or cold. Serve with crusty wholewheat bread and chunks of Cheddar cheese for a light supper.

●185 calories per portion

Radish and potato crunch

SERVES 4
1 lb new potatoes (see Buying guide)
salt
¼ cup butter
3 thick slices white bread, crusts removed and cut in ½ inch dice
2 inch piece of cucumber, diced
6 radishes, thinly sliced
2 tablespoons dry roasted peanuts
1 teaspoon chopped chives
freshly ground black pepper
¼ cup sour cream

1 Boil a saucepan of salted water and cook the potatoes for 15-20 minutes until just tender. ⚠ Drain well and, when cool enough to handle, cut in ½ inch dice. Let cool completely.
2 To make the croutons: Melt the butter in a skillet. When it is sizzling, add diced bread and sauté gently, turning as necessary, until golden. Drain the croutons well on absorbent kitchen paper. Let cool completely.
3 Place the diced potato, fried croutons, cucumber, radishes, peanuts and chives into a bowl. Season to taste with salt and pepper. Add the sour cream and mix gently. Serve at once, otherwise the salad will lose its crunch. ⚠

Cook's Notes

 TIME
Preparation, including cooking the potatoes and cooking the croutons, takes about 30 minutes. Allow 30 minutes for cooling. Fixing the salad takes 5 minutes.

 BUYING GUIDE
Choose a type of potato, such as Round Red or California Long White, which will not break up during cooking.

! **WATCHPOINTS**
Watch the potatoes carefully – they should be cooked through but still firm. If overcooked, they will break up instead of cutting into neat dice.

Mix gently so that the ingredients are thoroughly coated in the sour cream but remain separate.

 VARIATIONS
Add a small chopped green pepper instead of cucumber.

Omit the peanuts and sprinkle the top of the salad with toasted, slivered almonds.

● 310 calories per portion

Spinach crêpes

MAKES 8 CRÊPES
**6 oz spinach, stems and large
    midribs removed**
vegetable oil, for greasing

BATTER
1 cup all-purpose flour
½ teaspoon freshly grated nutmeg
salt
1 egg
½ cup milk
½ cup water

1 Put the spinach in a pan with only the water that clings to the leaves after washing and cook over moderate heat for 5 minutes until completely tender.

2 Drain the spinach well in a colander, pressing with a large spoon to extract as much moisture as possible, then chop it as finely as you can with a sharp pointed knife.

3 Make the batter: Sift flour, nutmeg and salt into a bowl, make a well in the center and add the egg, milk and water. Using a wire whisk, gradually draw the flour into the liquid and when the flour is completely incorporated, stir in the chopped spinach.

4 Heat a little oil in a 7 inch omelet pan. Remove from the heat, pour in 2 tablespoons of the batter and tilt the pan until the batter evenly covers the base.

5 Return to the heat and cook until the top looks dry and the underside is golden brown. Loosen the edge with a slim spatula and shake the pan, then toss the crêpe over and cook on the other side for a further 20-30 seconds until golden. Lift the crêpe onto a sheet of waxed paper.

6 Continue making crêpes in the same way, interleaving them with waxed paper. Stir the batter frequently and grease the pan with more oil as necessary.

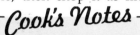

Cook's Notes

TIME
40 minutes preparation and cooking in total.

SERVING IDEAS
If wished the crêpes can be filled: Season 2 tablespoons cream cheese well with salt and pepper and spread on one end of each crêpe. Fold the sides over the filling, then roll up.

Alternatively, for a more substantial dish, fill the crêpes with about 1¼ cups well-flavored cheese sauce mixed with ¼ lb fried mushrooms or shelled shrimp.

✳ FREEZING
Cool completely, then wrap interleaved crêpes in foil, keeping them flat. Seal, label and freeze for up to 4 months. To serve: Thaw in wrappings, then unwrap and put on an ovenproof plate over a pan of simmering water. Cover and reheat for 5-10 minutes.

●90 calories per crêpe

Spinach special with lemon

SERVES 4
1½ lb fresh leaf spinach
1 teaspoon salt
2 tablespoons butter
2 tablespoons all-purpose flour
⅔ cup heavy cream
grated rind and juice of ½ lemon
freshly ground black pepper
pinch of freshly grated nutmeg
2 hard-cooked eggs, yolks and
    whites separated and finely
    chopped, for garnish

1 If using fresh spinach, thoroughly wash it in several changes of cold water to remove all the grit. Remove the stems and midribs and discard. Put the spinich in a large saucepan with just the water that adheres to the leaves after washing. ⨻ Sprinkle over the salt.
2 Cook the spinach over moderate heat for about 15 minutes, stirring occasionally with a wooden spoon. Turn the cooked spinach into a colander and drain thoroughly, pressing the spinach with a large spoon or a saucer to extract as much moisture as possible.
3 Melt the butter in the rinsed-out pan, sprinkle in the flour and stir over moderate heat for 3 minutes. Remove from heat, pour in the cream, and when it is completely blended, add the lemon rind and juice. ⨻ Season to taste with salt, pepper and nutmeg. Stir the spinach into the cream sauce and return to very low heat, just to heat through. ⨻
4 Turn the spinach into a heated serving dish and arrange the chopped hard-cooked eggs in rows over the top. Serve at once.

Cook's Notes

TIME
Preparation, if using fresh spinach, takes about 15 minutes. Cooking takes about 20 minutes.

WATCHPOINTS
It is best to cook spinach in its own juices – added water only makes it soggy.

Do not add lemon juice until butter, flour and cream are well blended. Otherwise, the acid will curdle the cream.

On no account allow the cream sauce to boil when heating through, or it will curdle.

BUYING GUIDE
If fresh spinach is not available, use 2 packages (10 oz each) frozen cut leaf spinach, thawed, and with all moisture pressed out. Stir into the sauce and cook 5 minutes.

●295 calories per portion

Spinach surprise

SERVES 4
1 lb fresh leaf spinach or 1 package (10 oz) frozen chopped spinach
salt
¼ cup margarine or butter
1 onion, minced
¼ cup all-purpose flour
⅔ cup milk
good pinch of freshly grated nutmeg
freshly ground black pepper
4 eggs, separated
1 tablespoon grated Parmesan cheese
margarine, for greasing

1 If using fresh spinach, wash very thoroughly and remove the stems and central midribs. Place the spinach in a saucepan with only the water that clings to the leaves, and sprinkle with salt. Cover and cook over moderate heat for about 10 minutes until the spinach is cooked, stirring occasionally. If using frozen spinach, cook according to package directions.

2 Drain the spinach well in a sieve, pressing out all the excess water. Chop the spinach, if using fresh. Grease a 6-cup soufflé mold with margarine. Preheat oven to 375°.

3 Melt the margarine in a large saucepan, add the onion and cook over low heat for about 5 minutes until soft and lightly colored. Sprinkle in the flour and stir over low heat for 1-2 minutes until straw-colored. Remove from the heat and gradually stir in the milk. Return to moderate heat and simmer, stirring, until thick.

4 Stir in the chopped spinach and grated nutmeg and season well with salt and pepper. Simmer over gentle heat for 2 minutes.

5 Remove from the heat. Beat the egg yolks and beat them into the spinach mixture.

6 Beat the egg whites until they are just standing in soft peaks then fold gently into the spinach mixture with a metal spoon. ⚠

7 Pour the mixture into the greased soufflé mold and sprinkle the top evenly with the grated Parmesan cheese. Bake in the oven for 30-40 minutes until risen and lightly browned on the top. It should be firm to the touch on the outside, and not wobbly if gently shaken, but still moist in the center. Serve at once straight from the dish.

Cook's Notes

 TIME
Preparation takes about 30 minutes, cooking 30-40 minutes.

SERVING IDEAS
This spinach dish is very versatile: Serve as a light lunch or supper or as an appetizer. Or try it as a vegetable accompaniment: It goes very well with veal or lamb dishes.

For individual soufflés, bake in four 1½-cup greased molds for 20-30 minutes, or eight 1-cup greased soufflé molds for 15-20 minutes.

⚠ **WATCHPOINT**
Do not overbeat the egg whites. It is easier to fold in the whites if you first beat 1-2 tablespoons of beaten whites into the spinach mixture to slacken it. Carefully fold in the whites so as not to lose the trapped air.

 VARIATION
For a more substantial main-course dish, add ½ cup finely chopped cooked ham or chicken.

●250 calories per portion

Sweet potatoes with ginger

SERVES 6
1 large sweet potato, weighing about 2 lb, cut in 1½ inch cubes (see Buying guide)
salt
¼ cup vegetable oil
1 tablespoon butter
1 teaspoon ground ginger
freshly ground black pepper

1 Preheat the oven to 400°.
2 Boil the potato cubes in salted water for about 7 minutes, until they are beginning to soften. ! Drain thoroughly.
3 Melt the butter in the oil in a roasting pan over moderate heat for about 2 minutes, until the mixture begins to turn a golden color.

4 Remove the pan from the heat, transfer the potatoes carefully into the hot oil, sprinkle with the ginger and salt and pepper. Roast in the oven for 45-60 minutes, turning occasionally, until golden brown.

Cook's Notes

 TIME
Preparation takes 15 minutes, including parboiling the potatoes, then 45-60 minutes roasting.

WATCHPOINT
Do not allow the sweet potatoes to become too soft when parboiling.

 BUYING GUIDE
Buy only as many sweet potatoes as you can use immediately, as they do not store well. They are nutritious vegetables, high in Vitamin A.
Although much sweeter tasting than ordinary potatoes, they are prepared and cooked in the same way.

 VARIATION
Cook sweet potatoes in the drippings around a meat roast as you would ordinary potatoes - the roasting time will vary, according to oven temperature.

SERVING IDEAS
Sweet potatoes go well with pork roast, ham or broiled chicken.

●185 calories per portion

Tomatoes with basil and cream

SERVES 4-6
6 ripe tomatoes (weighing about
    1 lb), halved
3 tablespoons olive oil
1 lb onions, thinly sliced
salt and freshly ground black
    pepper
1 tablespoon chopped fresh basil,
    or 1 teaspoon dried
⅔ cup light or sour cream

1 Cut an X on the cut sides of the tomato halves (see Cook's tip)
2 Heat the oil in a large skillet, add the onions and put the tomatoes, cut side uppermost, on top of the onions. Season well with salt and pepper and sprinkle the basil over the top.

3 Cook over gentle heat for 7-10 minutes until the tomatoes begin to soften. [!]
4 Carefully turn the tomatoes over with a slotted spatula and cook for about 5 minutes on the cut side.

5 Pour the cream over the tomatoes and onions and warm through gently, but do not let the mixture boil. Taking care not to split the tomatoes, transfer to a warmed serving dish and serve at once.

Cook's Notes

 TIME
Preparation and cooking take about 20 minutes.

 COOK'S TIP
Cutting an X in the tomatoes helps the heat penetrate evenly and prevents the tomatoes from splitting during cooking.

 WATCHPOINT
Do not let the tomatoes overcook or they will become mushy. They should just begin to soften, but still hold their shape. Cooking time will vary according to their ripeness and size.

 VARIATION
Try fresh or dried thyme instead of basil.

 SERVING IDEAS
This makes a rather special snack if served on sautéed or hot French bread.

●210 calories per portion

Tomatoes and cod in cider

SERVES 4

1¾ lb cod fillet, cut in 4 equal
    serving pieces, or 4 cod steaks,
    each weighing about 7 oz
¾ lb tomatoes
2 tablespoons butter
⅔ cup dry cider
salt and freshly ground black
    pepper
2 tablespoons chopped parsley
1 tablespoon chopped fresh thyme,
    or 2 teaspoons dried

1 Preheat the oven to 400°.
2 Cut one tomato in 4 slices. Scald,
peel and chop the rest.
3 Use a little of the butter to lightly
grease a shallow ovenproof dish.
Put the chopped tomatoes into the
dish and then place the pieces of
cod on top.
4 Put the remaining butter and the
cider into a saucepan over low heat
to melt the butter. Pour the mixture
over the cod.
5 Season the cod and scatter the
herbs over it. Put a tomato slice on
each piece of fish.
6 Bake the cod for 20 minutes or
until cooked through. Serve hot,
straight from the dish.

Cook's Notes

 TIME
This dish takes 40 mi-
nutes to make.

 COOK'S TIP
If using cod fillet, ask
the supplier to skin if
for you.

 VARIATION
For an equally tasty
version try haddock or
pollock.

●230 calories per portion

66

Watercress castles

SERVES 4
1 bunch watercress
salt
1 lb carrots, sliced
6 oz potatoes, cut in large chunks
2 eggs, beaten
freshly grated nutmeg
freshly ground black pepper
margarine, for greasing
carrot curls, for garnish (see
Preparation)

1 Heat the oven to 350° and then grease four 1-cup dariole molds (see Cook's tip).

2 Bring a pan of salted water to a boil, add the carrots and potatoes and cook them for about 20 minutes until they are soft.

3 Meanwhile, chop the watercress finely, reserving a few sprigs for decoration.

4 Drain the carrots and potatoes, return to the pan and set over low heat for 1-2 minutes to dry off any excess moisture from vegetables.

5 Allow the vegetables to cool slightly, then purée in a blender or a food processor until smooth. Transfer purée to a bowl and add the watercress and eggs. Season to taste with freshly grated nutmeg, salt and freshly ground pepper, then stir to mix well.

6 Divide the carrot purée between the molds and place them in a baking dish. Pour in enough boiling water to come halfway up the sides of the molds, then bake castles in the oven for 30 minutes or until they are firm.

7 Run a round-bladed knife around the edge of each mold and unmold carefully. Garnish with the reserved watercress sprigs and carrot curls and serve at once.

Cook's Notes

 TIME
These attractive molds take 40 minutes to make and bake in total.

 COOK'S TIP
If dariole molds are unavailable use tall cream caramel molds or improvise with ovenproof china tea cups or ramekin dishes that hold at least 1 cup.

 VARIATION
As an alternative to watercress, chopped fresh tarragon combines well with carrot.

 PREPARATION
To make carrot curls for the garnish:

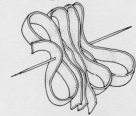

Using a potato peeler, pare strips off a carrot, then roll up and spear with cocktail wooden picks. Leave in ice water for 1 hour, then remove the sticks before use.

●105 calories per castle

Watercress and potato croquettes

SERVES 4-6
1½ lb potatoes
salt
2 tablespoons margarine or butter
2 tablespoons milk
freshly grated nutmeg
freshly ground black pepper
1 bunch watercress, finely chopped
2 eggs, beaten
flour, for dusting
½ cup finely chopped blanched
    almonds
4 tablespoons soft white bread
    crumbs
⅔ cup vegetable oil

FOR GARNISH
watercress sprigs
lime twists (optional)

1 Bring the potatoes to a boil in salted water, lower the heat and cook for 20 minutes.
2 Drain the potatoes and mash with the margarine and milk until smooth. Season to taste with nutmeg, salt and pepper, then beat in the watercress and about one-fourth of beaten eggs. Let the mix-ture cool for about 30 minutes.
3 Lightly dust a working surface with the flour. Divide the mixture into 12 portions then, with floured hands, roll into cork shapes.
4 Mix the almonds with the bread crumbs and spread out on a large flat plate. Dip the croquettes first in the remaining beaten egg, then roll in the almond and bread crumb mixture. Refrigerate for at least 30 minutes (see Cook's tip).
5 Preheat the oven to 225°.
6 Heat the oil in a large heavy-based skillet to 375° or until a dry bread cube turns brown in 50 seconds.
7 Cook a batch of croquettes in the hot oil for about 5 minutes, until golden brown and crisp, then re-move with a slotted spoon and drain on absorbent kitchen paper. Keep warm in the oven while cook-ing the rest of the croquettes. ✳
8 Garnish with watercress and lime twists, if liked, and serve.

Cook's Notes

 TIME
40 minutes preparation; 30 minutes each cooling and chilling and about 15 minutes cooking.

 FREEZING
Drain and cool the fried croquettes. Flash freeze until solid, then pack in rigid containers, separating layers with foil. Seal, label and return to freezer for up to 3 months. To serve: Thaw in a single layer on a baking sheet at room tempera-ture for 2 hours, then cover and reheat in a 350° oven for 20 minutes.

SERVING IDEAS
Serve as an interesting accompaniment to broiled or roast meat. Alterna-tively, serve as a light vegetarian snack with a salad.

COOK'S TIP
Chilling firms up the mixture, which helps to prevent the croquettes from breaking up during cooking. However, chilling is not abso-lutely necessary if you are short of time – just take extra care when cooking.

●410 calories per portion

68

Zucchini and cheese soup

SERVES 6
1 lb zucchini, cut in 1 inch lengths
3 ¾ cups chicken broth
1 mint sprig
2 tablespoons margarine or butter
1 onion, chopped
1 clove garlic, minced (optional)
¾ cup full-fat soft cheese (see Economy)
⅔ cup milk
salt and freshly ground black pepper

TO SERVE
6 ice cubes
2 tablespoons heavy cream (see Economy)
extra mint sprigs, for garnish

1 Put the zucchini into a large pan with the broth and mint sprig. Bring to a boil, then lower the heat and simmer for 10 minutes.

2 Meanwhile, melt the margarine in a small pan, add the onion and garlic, if using, and sauté gently for 5 minutes until the onion is soft and lightly colored.

3 Remove the zucchini from the heat and stir in the onion and garlic. Let cool slightly, then pour the zucchini mixture into a blender and work to a purée.

4 In a large bowl, blend the cheese with the milk a little at a time, then beat with a wooden spoon until smooth and creamy. Stir in the zucchini purée to mix well.

5 Pour the soup into a clean large bowl or soup tureen, cover and refrigerate for about 4 hours or overnight.

6 To serve: Season the soup to taste with salt and pepper (see Cook's tip) and divide between 6 individual soup bowls. Add ice cubes, swirl over the cream and garnish with mint. Serve at once.

Cook's Notes

TIME
15 minutes preparation, cooking time 10 minutes, then chilling for 4 hours or overnight.

VARIATION
Instead of zucchini, use 1 large cucumber cut in ¾ inch lengths.

ECONOMY
For a less expensive soup lower in calories, use a small-curd cottage cheese or Quark instead of full-fat cheese and plain yogurt instead of the heavy cream.

COOK'S TIP
Wait until the soup has chilled and the flavors have developed before adding the seasoning.

SERVING IDEAS
Served just with fresh rolls or crusty bread and butter, this soup makes a delicious lunch for a hot day.

●180 calories per portion

Zucchini mousse

SERVES 4-6
½ lb zucchini, sliced about ½ inch
   thick
2 tablespoons margarine or butter
⅔ cup thick bottled mayonnaise
⅔ cup cold chicken broth
2 eggs, separated
3 tablespoons water
2 envelopes unflavored gelatin
2 tablespoons chopped chives
few drops hot pepper sauce
   (optional)
salt and freshly ground black
   pepper
½ lb tomatoes peeled, seeded and
   diced (see Cook's tip)

FOR GARNISH
tomato slices
1 tablespoon chopped chives

1 Melt the margarine in a large skillet over low heat, add the zucchini and cook gently for about 15 minutes until soft, stirring so that the zucchini do not brown.
2 Place the zucchini with the mayonnaise, chicken broth and egg yolks in a blender or food processor and process to a purée.
3 Put the water in a bowl, sprinkle over the gelatin and leave to soak until spongy. Then stand the bowl in a pan of hot water and stir until the gelatin is dissolved and the liquid is clear.
4 Turn the purée into a large bowl and stir in the chives and the hot pepper sauce, if using. Taste and season. Then stir in the dissolved gelatin. Leave in the refrigerator for about 30 minutes until just setting.
5 Stir the purée until smooth then stir in the diced tomato. Beat the egg whites until they stand in stiff peaks and then carefully fold into the purée.

6 Turn the mixture into a 5-cup soufflé mold and chill for about 1½ hours or until set.
7 Serve garnished with tomato slices and chopped chives.

Cook's Notes

TIME
The mousse takes about 30 minutes to prepare, allow 30 minutes for the mixture to come to setting point in the refrigerator, plus the chilling time.

COOK'S TIP
When seeding the tomatoes, cut out the hard white piece of core under the stalk as it is rather dry and tough to eat and will spoil the texture of the mousse.

●355 calories per portion

Zucchini with onion and nuts

SERVES 4
1 lb zucchini
¼ cup butter
2 tablespoons water
salt
1 onion, sliced in rings
1 oz pine nuts (pignoli)
freshly ground black pepper

1 Cut the zucchini into quarters lengthwise, then cut across to make even-size sticks.

2 Melt half the butter in a saucepan with the water and a pinch of salt. Add the zucchini, cover the pan and cook gently for 10 minutes until the zucchini are just tender. Shake the pan occasionally during this time to ensure that they cook evenly.

3 Meanwhile, melt the remaining butter in a skillet, add the onion rings and cook briskly for 3 minutes until lightly browned. Transfer with a slotted spoon to a plate and set aside.

4 Add the pine nuts to the pan and sauté for 2 minutes, stirring, until golden brown.

5 Drain the zucchini, season to taste with salt and pepper, and transfer them to a warmed shallow serving dish. Arrange the onion rings down the center of the zucchini and sprinkle the pine nuts over the top.

Cook's Notes

 TIME
This easy-to-make vegetable dish takes only 20 minutes to prepare.

 SERVING IDEAS
A tasty way of serving zucchini as a vegetable accompaniment, this dish is excellent with any broiled or roast meat, poultry or fish.

 VARIATIONS
Green or English runner beans may be used instead of zucchini.

Replace the pine nuts with slivered almonds or walnut halves. Alternatively, replace the pine nuts with small cubes of crisply-fried bread.

●105 calories per portion.

INDEX

PICTURE CREDITS

Theo Bergstrom   Chris Knaggs

Martin Brigdale   Bob Komar

Alan Duns   Don Last   Tony Robins

Paul Forrester   Fred Mancini   Paul Webster

James Jackson   Peter Myers   Paul Williams

Paul Kemp   Roger Phillips   Graham Young